Be Still And Know…

You Are God

*   *   *

Use the Power Within To

Consciously Create Happiness And

The Life You Seek

Dan Keating

ISBN-10: **1481184989**
ISBN-13: 978-1481184984

www.dan-keating.com

To God

Whose ideas and inspiration made this possible and who gladly gave me His power and knowledge. His love was always there and His conversation continually urged me on.

I Thank You

To My Editor

Without this loving lady this book would not be what it is, from the bottom of my heart thank you.

Table of Contents

"What lies behind us and what lies before us are tiny matters compared to what lies within us."

Ralph Waldo Emerson

PROLOGUE

"You are God?" "How can one possibly say that? You must be deranged! You have got to be kidding."

Did words like those run through your mind? I can easily understand if they did. I would have said the same things many years ago. The statement "You are God or I am God" is not a statement I take lightly, nor did it come easily to me, nor from one mighty flash of inspiration. I do not believe it to be a statement of ego and is not meant to imply that *only* you are God, nor does it say you are *The* God. I believe *ALL* humans are God. We are in this together. It is the *nature* of who we really are. We are spiritual beings, having a human experience. (I will cover the subject of our human nature.) "You are God" is a statement about what Life is all about. And how many times have we all wondered just that? What is this all about?!

PLEASE NOTE one really important point that I wish to make up front. This book is not centered on any particular church or religion. It is not a comparison or discussion of their practices or "Holy" books. I am not trying to form a new religion.

I believe our culture errs if it uses the words "religion" and "church" synonymously. When a "religious" person is referred to, it is most generally assumed that person adheres to a particular faith system, when, in fact, it merely means he/she believes in a higher power. The majority of dictionaries I've checked show the first definition for the word "religion" as "belief in and reverence for a supernatural power or powers regarded as creator and governor of the universe." This definition does not begin to imply any specific faith, and certainly not a specific church. In other words, I am not coming from a "church" belief system or a specific faith. But I, most assuredly, come from a position of a belief in a higher power which is the creator of and governor of the universe.

I choose to use the name "God." Others use different names or descriptive words. . . Great Spirit, Creator, the Force, Universal Mind, Higher Self, Jehovah, etc. It is easier for me to use just one name. Please, don't feel I'm trying to imply that "God" is the only name that's appropriate. I don't believe that He/She/It cares a bit. I also use the personal pronoun "He." This is not meant to imply that God is of the male gender. I don't believe that to be so, but let's not complicate the issue.

Back to my audacious title. I wish to discuss with you what I believe to be the nature of God and the nature of humans, and how the two connect. I believe the understanding of that connection, becoming more aware of it, and using it to your advantage is what makes life better. I will talk about the Law of Creation and how our use of that law dictates what is happening to us, whether we like it or not.

I will also show you how I have used the tools of my beliefs to overcome disease and addiction, improve relationships, weave my way through challenges, and even find parking spaces on crowded streets. These creative methods are meant to improve *every* facet of your life.

You may come away from reading this book and still believe it ludicrous to believe We are God. That's perfectly OK! But I hope you will come away with strategies to re-think your life, if you feel it's necessary, and make improvements. I hope you will feel empowered, knowing that you have full control over any decisions you make. In order for you to make your life better, you have to feel better. We will work on making that happen.

Blessings to you.

There has to be a moment, a pinpoint in time, when we say, "Things have to be different." I now commit to making it different. Let this be that moment.

Dan Keating

Chapter 1
The Nature of God

In discussing the nature of God it is important to note the use of the verb *is*. *Is,* as I'm using it here, means the very being, essence, or nature of a thing. To say that God *is* something is not just a matter of using adjectives to describe Him. It is so much more than that. As an example, to say that God is love does not merely describe him as loving. It is a statement of what God's nature really is. Love is a word expressed to reveal God's very being.

God is Love

There are many aspects which intertwine to make up the whole of what God is. Love is the one I feel best describes the whole. Love, in this context, means *all* things positive, *all* things good, *all* things that would be of no harm. God is Perfect Love.

Perfect Love is without conditions or judgments, an Impersonal Love. God plays no favorites. Every human is regarded equally by God, without prejudice or bias of any kind. God's love is limitless, for that is what He *is*. It will never run out. This love is present in, and *is*, everything created by God. God is omnipresent. . .therefore, His Love is omnipresent.

Humans describe love somewhat differently. We can express love in impersonal ways, but most often our understanding of love is as an emotion of strong personal attachment and affection. Human beings have not yet fully discovered how to express love impersonally as God does. Impersonal Love can also be expressed using other human words like joy, happiness, harmony, and peace.

God is Intelligence

God is Intelligence itself, the intelligence that designed our planet, our galaxy, our specific universe, and all other universes. God's creation is a vast and complex system. The human mind has not yet come close to figuring out the totality of it or how it all operates. However, vast though it is, our universe operates within a series of Universal Laws. These laws keep our universe growing and expanding, in complete harmony.

While our various sciences have done much through the ages to explain this universe, we still have far to go. In human terms, if we were to try to describe an intelligence capable of creating our universe, we would call that being a super, super genius, logically needing an intelligence we do not comprehend. All physical creation was Divinely created.

Of course, not everyone believes in the theory of creation. I believe we live in an evolutionary environment, but could it have come from nothing? Show me any material object you can hold in your hand and tell me that it could have come from nothing. And this is a material universe. Does it not seem logical that some law is in effect? Everything evolved from a creative process, an intelligent process...ideas. I will discuss that creative process later.

The planet earth is the most complex environment yet found by us. Our environment operates within a series of laws. These laws keep our environment operating in perfect harmony, without any need for human intervention. An example would be gravity. The harmony of our universe, the way everything works as it should, could most certainly imply Intelligence of a very high order.

God is Life

God does not merely *give* life. He *is* Life. He is your life, and He is my life. Life is being or existence. That would be pretty inclusive of *everyone* and *everything*, wouldn't it?

Life is energy. God created the universe from the one substance that is present everywhere, including that of Himself. That one substance is energy. Everything seen and unseen is energy. There is nowhere that energy is not; it is omnipresent. Every atom, and that which is even smaller, is made from this energy. God is, therefore, everything; and everything is one with everything else, including Man.

Our earth environment is teeming with life, and every cell in all life contains God's energy. God is all things living, like trees, flowers, the animals and the decaying forest floor. He is the lightning that starts forest fires and the fire. God is all things that we usually call non-living but which contain His energy and His life force, items like rocks, sand, water, and aluminum. All life *is* God, given by God, and made of God-stuff. *We are God.*

God is Power

Power is deemed to be possessed by those in authority. As the creator of all there is, God is considered to be the total authority in the universe. This Power is one of strength or dominion and does not suggest coercion or duress. God's Power is an impersonal power, which He gives freely and lovingly to anyone desiring to use it. His Power works through our life, whether we are aware of it or not. Divine Power is unlimited possibilities with limitless potential. God's Power is the *creative force* which gives us ideas and allows us to experience whatever we want.

God is Soul

This is an aspect of God that is most important for us humans to realize, to become aware of. Soul is God within each one of us. Soul is that *personal connection* to God, from which we came and will return, when our human life is ended and our body decays. It is the infinite part of us, and it will live forever. The Soul is a personal fragment of God. A human analogy would be to say that God is the ocean, and the Soul is a drop of water from that ocean. The water drop contains all that the ocean is. The Soul contains everything that is God.

God is Truth

Truth is that which is. God is not merely truthful but Truth itself, absolute and unchangeable, at all times and in all circumstances.

In God's dimension only truth exists. In our human dimension we live in a world of duality, where there are opposites. The opposite of truth is falsehood. Our lives contain a great deal of falsehood, much of which is simply made up of false belief. Humans will go to war over a falsehood just as fast as they will go to war over truth and justice.

The God within has the truth for each human being. Written or spoken truth is often false. When we rely on God's Power and Wisdom, we can better tell the difference between truth and falsehood. As we increase our awareness of God and our practice of God's presence within us, falsehood does not visit our lives nearly as often. When we are in the presence of truth, falsehood stands no chance.

God is Wisdom

God's Wisdom is the storehouse of *all* knowledge and every event that has ever happened. Imagine for a moment a giant hard drive. If you are not into computers, you can imagine a universal encyclopedia. This hard drive contains all the knowledge of everything that has ever been. . .every memory, every event, every feeling. At the same time, it contains every possibility.

This storehouse of wisdom is also called Universal Consciousness. Have you ever given any thought to ideas? Where do they come from? Humans seem to come up with fantastic, new ideas all the time. Ideas come from Universal Consciousness. Another explanation might be that they come from God's Mind. God is this wisdom. From God's mind to your mind. . .same Mind. . .there is only one Mind. This wisdom is yours to use, and we will talk about how to access it.

The meaning of God's Wisdom goes further than what we would acknowledge to be accumulation of knowledge. In order to better understand God's Wisdom, I believe we have to add the aspect of Love to the equation. On a human level, we would probably all agree that an elder might have accumulated much, much knowledge over his lifetime, in any given subject. He might be able to recite a multitude of facts back to us. But it's his nature, his character, that makes him wise, not merely those facts. He might have a number of personal issues in his life. He might have made many decisions that pretty well messed up is life. Would we consider him wise just because he had a lot of "book learning?" He might be wise in his "head knowledge," but is he a wise person?

God's Love is inherent in His Wisdom. He guides each of us with something far beyond the accumulation of knowledge.

What God is Not

In trying to communicate what God *is*, it can help to also look at what God is *not*.

God is not hate. He does not hate anything. He especially does not hate you. He is incapable of hate or wrath, as it is not in His nature. We have created the belief in hate only in our human existence. Hate is merely the *absence* of love.

God is not needy. If God is all there is, how could he need anything? Furthermore, if he is Perfection, he would *need* no adoration or obedience from you. That, again, would imply he was somehow incomplete. I did not say that adoration or obedience were not good. They are! And our lives would be in better places if we practiced them. But they are not good *because* God *needs* them. There is a huge difference.

God is not vengeful. As His very being is Love, there is no room for revenge or desire to punish. There could be no plan in His heart for His children to be tormented after their physical death, because they had not done what was asked of them. We, as human parents, would certainly not threaten our children with eternal punishment. As a human, you might be frustrated and even angry, but *eternal punishment*? Or would you allow some other entity to do it? (Satan!)

Regardless of what you read in holy books or are told by holy men, God would have no need to punish, kill, or annihilate his creation. Hell is a figment of someone's imagination. It has been used as a threat for thousands of years. If you have been raised with the belief that you have to perform certain things or establish specific beliefs, in order to be saved from eternal punishment, examine those beliefs. Sometimes, we truly need to question authority. I'm not referring to God's authority. I refer to man's authority. The belief in a vengeful God has caused much fear and anguish on this earth.

God does not have a human rating system, like excellent, good, better, best, or holy, holier, holiest. All human beings, no matter who they are, are equal in God's eyes. Personal position on earth is of no consequence to God. No human is more holy than another, no matter what title has been given him/her. There are no "chosen people." All humans are chosen. No religious order, sect, or belief is better than another. No Holy Book is better than another.

God does not judge. He does not keep score or give bad marks. God gives and *is only* Love. God does not tally what we call sin. Sin is tallied by humans and exists only in the human mind.

God does not ever lose his patience. God *is* patience, and it is infinite. You can act like a reprobate until the day you die, and God will still hold eternal patience, waiting for you to realize who you really are, One with Him. There is a Universal Plan that might speak for reincarnation of some sort, and you will have an eternity to "get it right." When I say "might speak for reincarnation," I mean that I do not know what that Eternal Plan might be, but there has to be something beyond this one life I'm living now. God is not unfair, and there is a consistent fairness in the idea of reincarnation.

Knowing and understanding the nature of God will give you a needed awareness of that which you are a part. Having that awareness can then lead to a better you and a better world. Making your personal world better automatically makes the entire planet earth a better place. Further, with this awareness, you can practice bettering *your* world in the comfort, convenience, and privacy of your own human body and mind

We humans tend to concentrate on the negative aspects of life. We focus so much on negative feelings and events, we can find it

17

easy to assume those same tendencies of God. We might have had personal relationship difficulties with our earthly father, so we transfer our negative feelings to coincide with a belief in what God's nature is. A God with the nature discussed above would not have the *ability* to express the negative feelings or tendencies we think are natural. (That notion would support the idea that negative feelings are not *natural*, spiritually speaking. . .only *normal*, in human terms.)

Chapter 2
Where is God?

God has no home or residence, as humans define the word. God does not live in a place but rather is simply *in everything, everywhere*. There are no exceptions. That states it pretty simply. But, all of us think differently, perceive differently, believe differently and have different opinions about what various words mean. Therefore, I will state the same thing in many different ways, so you get a full understanding of what I am trying to say.

We see God everywhere we could possibly look. I see God every morning. I see Him in my wife's eyes. I see him in the bathroom mirror. I see him driving on the local streets. He works in the office buildings, the convenience store. He works the fields and grows the vegetables.

God lives in a small house overlooking the landfill. He is the house. He also has a home in a cardboard box or a tent. He lives in a Beverly Hills mansion. He is the mansion. God is all homes and all places.

In the far reaches of the universe, at distances and places that are yet to be imagined by humans, God is there. In the smallest particle in existence, which has yet to be discovered by scientists, God is that particle. God is in every cell of every human on earth, all seven billion of us. He just discovered a new technological thing-a-ma-jig. He discovered the human genome and hits golf balls 350-plus yards. God is the mother of the child and the child. He is the father playing baseball with his son and is also the baseball, the glove, and the son. God is the young girl at the mall with her friends, all of whom are also God. God is one minute old and also one instant from physical death, thousands of times each and every day.

God comes in all sizes and colors, and He speaks every language. No matter what an individual thinks or believes, God *is* that human. That person can be a lover, a hater, or just kind of mean. He/She is still God. This includes those human beings that we believe caused us, individually or as a society, great personal harm, people like Hitler, Stalin, Genghis Kahn and thousands of others. God lived as Jesus, Buddha, Saint Francis, Mother Theresa, and He presently lives as you.

God is the human who blows up other people, as well as the people being blown up. God is the U.S. Marine on patrol, as well as the person he is hunting. God lives on death row. He is the killer, the robber, the drug pusher, and the one pursuing them. He is the starving child in Africa and the lost hiker on the mountain.

God is in everything. The rings of Saturn are God. The heat of the sun is God, too. What you cannot see, whether it be in the depths of space or in a breath of air on your cheek, that is God. A child running through the cool water from a yard hose is God experiencing pure joy. He is the wet grass her feet touch. He is the water that splashes on the child and the butterfly flying around her head.

God is the life energy and natural intelligence that grows an oak tree from a small acorn. When the flower blooms, you see Him in His finest clothes. He is also in the rock and the mud on your shoes. He is the snake, the horse, and "man's best friend."

God is the virus and the bacteria, as well as the cancer cell. God is the radiation that kills the cell and the nutrition which prevents the cell from forming. He is the energy in every cell of each individual human body. All that makes up the cell, is God. There is space between all cells, and that is God, too.

God is in all matter, seen and unseen. Every molecule of our universe is God. The entirety of it is God *experiencing, expressing His Life through each of us*. God *is* all Life and provides all Life to everyone, with the inherent *free will* to live it whatever way he/she chooses to experience it. With that free will you might choose to experience baking a cookie. You might choose to hurt someone. You could prefer writing a check to the local food bank. It is *ALL* God, experiencing His Life.

No matter where you turn or what or who you look at, that is God. There is nowhere that God is not. *You are God and So Am I.*

There are no exceptions to the "everything, everywhere" rule.

Chapter 3
Why We Are Here

Question: Why are we here?

Answer: To be God in perfect human form.

God's original idea

God's original idea, was to experience all of his Power, Wisdom, and Love in an existence other than the one He *is*, which is a realm of pure, perfect energy. He chose to create an environment and an apparatus by which He could experience everything that was not available in an environment of perfection. God's desire was to experience Himself in human form, through each one of us.

The awesome and profound idea of this human existence is this: In God's plan for our human existence, he individualized the Spirit that *is* Him. (Note the root meaning of the word "individualized": *un*-divided. Dictionaries might actually define the word as meaning "separate." But "undivided" is "undivided.") We are individuals, and we are One with God. There is an obvious dichotomy here. How can we be both? We just *are both,* as the water drop *is* water. . .one individual drop. . .part of what we know to *be water.* Again, the water drop is water. *We Are God.* Not "separate" in our very nature. Our *real, inherent, authentic, indestructible* nature is Spirit. We are *spirit* beings living in a *human* body. (The nature of the human will be covered in a later chapter.)

Equally as awesome is the Perfect Love Idea, that we have *free will*. We are God, with *all* His unlimited, unfathomable capabilities (despite the fact that we don't know it and don't live it). ***When we allow Him***, he will provide all that is good for us, in every aspect of our life. That is unqualified. . .*ALL THAT IS GOOD*. Furthermore, all that is good includes a body in perfect form, not aging or deteriorating. We have human minds, our so-called ego, that part of us that believes we are all separate beings. With the gift of free will we are able to think any kind of thought we wish, choose any experience we want. Otherwise, free will would have no meaning. And if it were otherwise, we would merely be the puppets of a Higher Power, with no choice in our being, at the whim of some kind of "destiny." Having said this, the questions might logically arise, "How can you say I chose these horrible things that have happened to me? Why would I do that?" Legitimate questions. The process of creation, and how we use it's power, will also be covered in a later chapter.

As humans, we are here as actors in the play of life on the planet earth. The play of life can be compared to a movie, TV show, or stage play. God is in the role of director, and you and I are the actors. This, however, is not the typical entertainment production. In the play of life we (each for himself) design which character we are going to play, as well as the script that character will follow, all achieved by our choices. We also have the option of changing the character and/or the script at any time. One minute you can be a saint, and the next you can be a dark, evil villain. As a saint you can help save the world, and as the villain you can destroy the world, and other actors as well. You can even choose to destroy the character you have chosen to play. The theater and the sets are already done and waiting for your use. If you do not like the sets, they can be changed, too. The theater can also be changed by the action of the characters, but this takes the participation of a great many characters together to accomplish. You have the freedom to play an unlimited number of roles and write an unlimited number of scripts. (Career change? Divorce? Different scripts.)

In any role we choose to play there is one constant. The character we choose, *every* character, is always God. Although our personalities, our character, and our actions don't always appear to be so, *We Are God*, experiencing. This never stops, until we return to the non-physical (spiritual) realm from which we came. Each of us is a character created solely to play a part of God. As individualized God, we each choose the character we are to be, and we choose our own script (life).

As actors we need not pay any conscious attention to the Director. (Remember, that free will thing.) We can choose to *consciously* play the role, with God's direction, and experience Him in perfect human form. Because of our free will, if we choose to disregard the direction, we will not be fired or punished. The Director will not think less of us or threaten us in any way. And this Director never judges. If we make a mistake, we simply start again. As actors participating in this play, the only contract agreed upon is our choice to play a human being. We can cancel our contract at any moment we choose. As the Director, God directs one way, impersonally, positively, and lovingly. He gives all His Power, Wisdom, and Love continuously. It is up to the actors to decide if they wish to use it or not. By choosing a script of our own ego self, we will, to whatever degree, experience a life of chaos, disruption, illness, and fear.

*   *   *

We are here to experience life. God Himself expresses only love, but He created our world of duality so that He can experience opposites, including love or fear, through us. The human form was designed to have this ability on purpose, for the experience of choice. Because we are God, we intuitively lean toward love. But if any of us choose to express fear, or anything negative, there is no judgment, not on God's part. We are allowed to create whatever type of life we wish, and there is no Divine punishment. We may be punished by ourselves or our fellow humans, but never by God.

History and observation show that for millennia we have been experiencing the fear side of the world of duality. This could change as quickly as the next moment. When we choose to express love rather than fear, we will then experience that love, in its many forms; and our society will be different. By *deliberately* choosing love, by ripple effect, our earth will be changed.

And that is the "why" of our life. . .to do what God would do and to be what God is, all of which is good beyond measure. We are all coming to that realization, whether we state it that way or understand it that way, or not. We are *becoming* Who We Really Are, and we each are doing it at our own rate of speed and in our own way. Ain't it great?

Chapter 4
Spirit Manifests As Human

If you are God and I am God, then it would have to be that we were *all* included in the process of creating the universe, and our planet earth. All of Spirit, all of God, created this phenomenon. My words are *never* intended to imply separation. So when I refer to God's creation, God's idea or plan, I always intend the inclusion of us *all* in that discussion. Hence, I am referring to God as the *All* That Is.

*   *   *

All creation starts with an idea. God's idea originated as a thought in His consciousness. God's consciousness was and is the source of all ideas, knowledge and wisdom. As you will recall, the original idea was for God to experience all of His Power, Wisdom, and Love in an existence beyond just a concept, an existence of experience.

God took His idea of our universe, as well as our planet and human life on it, and molded it into an intense creative desire. Using this intense desire, He combined it with His power, wisdom, and love. The original idea expanded and refined, until the entire idea was completely formed as a crystal-clear picture in God's Universal Mind (what we would call visualization). God spoke the word of creation, which then became the frequency vibration, commanding his desire to take form. It was God's Law, at this point, that this vision *had* to manifest. Holding His vision firmly in Universal Mind, knowing that His idea was complete, the frequency created by His word attracted the exact set of matching vibrations necessary to combine the correct energy frequencies, and the manifestation of our universe began. God was the cause; the universe was the effect.

Albert Einstein postulated such and in the 1930's said, *"Everything is energy and that's all there is to it. Match the frequency of the reality you want and you cannot help but get that reality. It can be no other way. This is not philosophy; this is physics."*

God's vision, complete to the smallest detail, contained everything needed to create the universe. . .the planets, stars and suns, as well as black holes, nebula, and super novas. Included was the environment necessary for the process of evolution of all life on our specific planet. As time went by, and life evolved, millions of forms manifested. These forms included hundreds of thousands of varieties of trees and plants, plus all the varieties of animal species that would eventually give all God-Beings infinite experiences. Also needed were land and water creations of such immense beauty and variety that they would constantly give us joy and peace. In addition, the vision included all of the natural food sources that would be necessary to keep man alive and in perfect health.

God's creation began to manifest piece by piece, element by element. Once it began, it has continued, and still continues. The universe is so vast and well-designed it could keep us busy for an infinite number of years, creating and discovering new ways to experience life.

Our specific physical universe is close to 14 billion years old, and planet earth is approximately 4.5 billion years old. Life started on earth about 4 billion years ago, according to our science. As you can see, in earth years this has been a rather long process, but the results have been spectacular.

In order to experience the original idea, we created the human body as the device to carry that part of God we call soul or spirit. Both the notions of human evolution and divine creation are true. We were with God, all of us being Spirit, when He created the universe, using both His divine creative power and the evolutionary process. God created the universe and is everything, everywhere; all creation is divine and continues to evolve.

At some point along the way (we don't know when) the spirit, or soul, began coming into human forms and began thinking and creating at a level not ever seen on earth up until that time. Before we came to the earth environment as souls, we expressed and experienced only in conceptual form and only in the realm of spirit. God is all power, wisdom, and love; and, as such, we had the *idea* of human experience in all its manifestations, but not the actual physical experience of it. As God in the non-physical, we are conceptual beings and express only concepts. In this conceptual dimension God is pure energy.

In the earth environment there were a small number of developing humanoids that the first souls entered. The bodies were chosen by us in soul form and became the first of us, as God, to express and experience in human form on earth. The humans continued to develop through the evolutionary process, just as all the other life forms on the planet did. All life, as well as the planet, is continually evolving and changing. These first souls entering physical bodies were entering fully-developed bodies. As children were born to these first souls, the newly-entering souls came into the body somewhere between conception and when the infant took its first breath. The time of entry is the choice of the individual soul.

The first souls had no past physical experience with operating in a human body. The humanoid body, of course, didn't need the soul to function at the level of instinct, but with a soul it became immediately more advanced than any other animal. The humanoid of that time was operating on its animal instinct and was exclusively concerned with survival. With soul in place, humans were now self-aware, but only to a point. Man's self-awareness was not very developed and took a back seat to the animal portion for many thousands of years. (Perhaps our sciences will someday be able to tell us how long that was.)

Upon the souls' entrance, humans innately had available to them all the power, wisdom and love, which is God, and all that this inherently meant. However, the human was not aware of it. Essentially, because Spirit is God and is with God, and knew perfection before leaving the perfect realm, it was really a matter of *forgetting* those abilities and gifts. (Humanity's true purpose is to *remember* Who We Really Are, God, and *deliberately* experience that perfection.)

As humans we manifested only rudimentary creative abilities. With the inspiration of God's ideas, knowledge, and wisdom, human development took a giant step forward. However, our egos and animal portions did not realize where the ideas and thoughts came from, as we started down the path of human development. Creation at this time was by default, or by accident, and was primarily based in fear, our animal instinctive behavior. *Deliberate* creation did not begin until much later.

In the beginning humans would have had no consciously-remembered life history. Imagine having no conscious experience of any kind of history. The humans now imbued with Divine

Spirits, were still so busy trying to survive they at first had no awareness of any kind of a relationship with a Higher Power. However, being spiritual beings, Man now had a mindful access to God that no other creature had. (We had that innate ability because we were God, but we had forgotten.)

God has been with everyone from the start. Over the eons some began to develop a spiritual awakening, or quickening, asking the questions, "where did we come from" and "where are my thoughts coming from?" There is evidence that people could have been doing this about 45,000 years ago, but quite possibly it has been much longer than that. In the last few thousand years more people have experienced high levels of spiritual awareness and have shared this awareness and knowledge. At the same time, primitive stories, passed down from generation to generation, were created to explain Man's interpretation of the answers to these questions. This is how mythologies were developed. There was an instinctual (God-given) need to understand their world and their place in it.

There is, as most scientists would say, a harmony inherent in our universe and on our planet. Is it necessary that there is an Intelligence behind this harmony? The answer has always been debated. Would harmony have come about by itself, through evolution? Would it have to be a plan?

There are "laws of nature." How did those laws come about? There would also seem to be action inherent in the evolutionary process. I contend if there is action, something had to initiate that action. The notion of initiation would necessarily imply Mind. But the Mind of a Higher Being? A human ego mind or even a group of minds is just not equipped to be the creator of something as complicated as life.

Life will continue, in some way, no matter how we believe it began. But there is so much of it that is so overwhelmingly beautiful, and evokes such love and appreciation in me; I find it impossible to believe that a greater intelligence with feelings of even greater love isn't what initiated life in the first place.

Chapter 5
Human Nature
The Material Body

A new human body begins when an egg and a sperm unite, creating a union of energy, which develops and grows, using its own innate intelligence. This intelligence is an individual portion of God's Universal Intelligence. Every cell, from birth until the death of the physical body, is an energy-producing entity. This energy system is Life. This energy is God, as He manifests in the human.

The human body was designed to operate in perfect, natural harmony with its surroundings, using its own built-in energy system. The body is a self-contained energy dynamo and needs no help, outside of air, water and nutrition. It needs no conscious thought to operate perfectly. The heart is the best example of the energy system making up our bodies; because its action can be measured and calibrated, using machines powered by electricity to measure the heart's electric current. And, again, it beats without conscious thought. Another example: after sleeping for eight hours, you awaken in the morning, refreshed and ready to go. Your body did everything necessary to rest and rejuvenate itself, with no effort or conscious thought from you. This is the energy system, powered by the innate Intelligence of God.

The role of the human body is simple. It is a carrier for the soul, which is that God part of us. This is what allows God to *experience* human life, which was the intent of His original idea. As God, we designed our human body and the environment for our chosen roles, which I have compared to actors in a play. We are all different and unique characters in this play. The human being has unlimited possibilities within whatever role is chosen. This allows the experience to be human *and* Divine, at the same time.

The human body is the most complex organism on earth. It was designed to operate extremely efficiently for hundreds of years and has the ability to heal itself when injured. As science has told us, the total of our cells are regenerated every seven years. This would indicate we shouldn't even be manifesting the aging process as we do. *We have new bodies every seven years.*

The construction of the human body has all the many movement skills necessary in order to survive. Today, however, it does not require all of the same physical skills for survival that it once did, particularly because our food sources are quite different. We also are more advanced technically, which allows people to choose many more ways to experience life, in different body forms than were possible before the technical advances. Many years ago, if you were severely injured, you would have most likely died; whereas, today you can survive and experience life in an altered body state. In this state you still have numerous different possibilities for experience. Again, it is your choice how you manipulate the possibilities.

The brain is the organ of the body that acts like an advanced super computer. The brain is an energy- and electrically-driven organ that runs the physical body with such precision that man himself has yet to scratch the surface in learning how it operates. The brain also appears to have the function of a temporary memory device, storing all the events and situations that happen to us during our lifetime. I say "appears to," because science is still in a quandary; and no one really knows where memory is stored or how information is physically retrieved. Science rarely considers anything other than those theories which can be physically tested. Universal Consciousness, or God, is rarely considered to be a possible answer.

But, what if the brain is actually the fastest data retrieval device that can be imagined; and all thoughts, ideas, and memories are really stored on an even more powerful super computer, which we can call God's Mind or Universal Consciousness? What if this information is stored as energy, and everyone can retrieve any of the information at will, no matter where it originated, his or her mind, or someone else's? Consciousness studies have shown that Universal Consciousness stores all information that has ever been, in an energy-like data base.

The evolution of life, including the human body, has taken millions of years to reach the present point. This did not happen by accident. The entire universe, the planet earth, and the human body were designed and created by a Super Intelligence to play the role of God, experiencing on a physical level. This entire colossal, beautiful, and amazing production is being carried out on the stage called earth and is entitled "God's Human Life." Without the human body and all its abilities, the experience could not be accomplished, as it was originally intended.

The human body is the apparatus that allows God to experience Himself in every form of human creativity, using every aspect of Man's body, mind, and spirit. At the same time, humans are capable of being perfect, as the God we are.

Chapter 6
Human Nature
The Personality

As you will recall, God's original idea was to experience Himself in all possible forms of human expression. God knew every possibility inherent in this, but only in conceptual form. Now, He would experience Himself in physical form.

When we began the human experience many thousands of years ago, our God-Selves were "babes in the woods," so to speak. We were Perfect Spirit, created by, as, and of God, but newly imbued in human form. We were God, the *real* us being Spirit. But, simultaneously, we were creatures who had recently been operating only instinctually. As human beings, we could not see, feel, or recognize our God-Selves, because we were wearing what I call the *mask* of human personality.

As God, we created the world of duality, necessary in the dimensions of time and space. A world of duality has, inherent to it, opposites. Love has its opposite, fear. Up has its opposite, down. Peace has its opposite, chaos. And, implicit in the law of opposites, is the God-given freedom of choice, free will. Along with the freedom of choice comes the law of cause and effect. Every choice, decision, and event has a cause and an effect. The world of duality is ruled by this law.

This mask of personality is made up of three portions, two of which are the *animal* portion and the *ego* portion. In the beginning these two portions of the mask completely covered the third part of the human personality, the **spiritual** portion. Through the eons of human life, to whatever degree we have chosen, we have allowed this mask to cover the spiritual side of our human personality. It has always been there, but many have become habituated in our belief that this world of duality is the only *real* world. Our choice has been to fully experience this duality, always with the power to decide what we want. We have to see the effect of what we don't want, in order to know what we do want.

Through recorded history, human personality has been studied by the ancient Chinese, Arabic, and Greek philosophers, starting in about 1700 BCE, until the present time. Many academics of today still rely upon very old philosophical and psychological studies done in the 1700's and 1800's.

The most recognizable person from the era of the late 1800s and early 1900s is Sigmund Freud, an Austrian considered to be the founding father of psychoanalysis. I like his description of the three aspects of human personality the best. Freud's original names for the three aspects were: the "it," the "I," and the "over I." It is simple and straight forward. His translator used the Latin forms, when translating from Freud's German, and they became "id," "ego," and "super-ego."

The id is the *instinctual* portion of man and is also called the *animal* portion of personality. The ego is the *reality* portion. This portion is thought to be responsible for our awareness of self as an individual. Self-awareness and, therefore, ego was only recognized by Man after the humanoid received the super-ego portion, which I call soul or spirit. The super-ego, in Freud's definition, is the *moral character*, also equated with the *spiritual* aspect of Man. The super-ego is a simple explanation of Man's divine nature.

At the point when the super-ego (Spirit) entered the humanoid, Man became both human and divine. God, through us, began His physical experience. Spirit, or super-ego, is that which gives man the aspect that makes him God. Without super-ego there is no ego, or self-awareness; and without self-awareness we would be classified as animals.

The mask of duality covered the super-ego so efficiently that we did not have the awareness that we were God, truly a matter of "forgetting" who we really were. This was done by design. If we had had immediate total realization that we were divine in the beginning, it would have overwhelmed our systems, mentally, psychologically, and physically. God wanted to physically experience every detail of human life, including the most primitive forms of human nature.

I have tried to describe the human personality in general terms, briefly discussing its three aspects. Now we will move on to discuss these three aspects in more detail, in order to give us a little more understanding of what makes us human and what makes us think and act the way we do. Hopefully, this will, in turn, help us to understand that we can make changes. If we are in any way dissatisfied with pieces of our lives, we can take deliberate, positive steps to obtain improvements.

Chapter 7
Human Nature
The Animal

Before the time of the first soul's arrival into physical form, humanoids were a high form of animal, but still an animal. They operated the same as animals still do today, by pure instinct. It is hard to imagine today what it was really like millions of years ago. We do have some evidence, but there is so little that the available picture is unclear. Humanoids have been on the planet for millions of years, and without the survival instinct we would not have made it. Science today is stating that the species homo evolved, and it is about 2.5 million years old. Further, they say that anatomically-speaking, our human forms are about 200,000 years old. Man, as a human being with a soul, has been around for a very long time, and as an animal for millions of years.

Man's animal survival instinct or, as Freud called it, the "id" portion of personality, is unconscious (not self-conscious) by definition. This portion does not judge, but functions only from complex animal responses. The id does not know good or evil and does not seem to have any awareness of duality, as do other parts of the personality.

Although no one really fully understands the animal portion of our brain, it has been shown that this portion directs the instinctual processes of the body. The human body operates by itself, with no help from anyone. Our heart beats, our lungs breathe, our body sweats, and our hair grows. Some power guides all the body's functions automatically. Before Spirit entered the humanoid body, these functions were present in all creatures of the animal kingdom. These functions have been in existence for well over 200 million years.

I believe this innate power to be that part of God's Intelligence that appears in you and me, and *all* life forms. As intricate and complex as life on earth is, I cannot imagine or believe it created itself spontaneously, or through accidental evolution. This is a design that took a creative, intelligent, divine mind. And, even though I am a part of it as a divine being, I still have a problem getting my head around it. The more I learn about our universe and our bodies, the more mind-boggling it seems. What we see as this life on earth is truly awesome and amazing.

Included in the physical functions of the body, the animal portion also seems to be in charge of our libido. As an animal, this is nothing more that the survival instinct. As a human, with the addition of the Spirit and ego portions of personality, Man becomes extremely unique, in comparison to other species and life forms. This uniqueness is demonstrated by the fact that the libido can change from a simple survival device to an entirely different aspect, one of pleasure. When you take the animal portion and add the creativity and desire for pleasure in the human personality, it becomes something far beyond just procreation. It becomes a many-varied cause of human experience, with far-reaching effects.

The function of the animal portion of the personality is also evident in the human child, when it is first born. Although this new being is barely removed from his/her pure perfection of

Spirit, for a short while he/she operates *primarily* from the animal portion of his/her personality. The child behaves like other animals would, distressed if hungry or otherwise uncomfortable, existing mostly from his/her needs for survival, by eating, drinking, and pooping. (It should go without saying that the infant is obviously not physically able to satisfy these needs for survival beyond these functions. But. . . there, I said it anyhow.)

There will be further discussion about the child and how his/her personality develops. The animal in man is capable of all aggressive behaviors represented in nature. This includes all animals. There are said to be about 2% to 3% of humans who, at one point or another, display these tendencies. Such occurrences, however, are growing fewer in number with each passing decade.

The influence of the animal portion of our personalities has decreased as humans have evolved. This doesn't mean we don't still have the instinct to survive. That will be a part of us for some time to come, to the degree that we believe our physical body's death is the end of "life." Our overall human evolution has brought us to the point of no longer having to live for survival alone. Most of us have learned to have faith that our survival is a little more secure.

Statistics show that violence is decreasing. Our increased self-awareness, that we are something more than just skin and bones, is probably responsible; although there are those scientists who say we are just smarter. Inclusive in this awareness would be our growing realization that we are all one; we are in this life together. We are thinking and believing more and more that we are one global family, not just a number of separate tribes. (The communication technologies we have created, of course, contributed immensely to this.) When this is coupled with our innate divine intelligence and the constant expression of God's power, wisdom, and love working in and through us, we will get better and better with each passing day. Every time we make the choice to express love rather than fear and violence, we take one step closer to becoming one loving community called earthlings. Through the whole amazing process, we are forever God, expressing life at every point along the way.

Chapter 8
Human Nature
Ego

Ego has only one true function. It was created to mask our spiritual nature. God designed the ego to allow Himself (Us) to experience *every* aspect of being human. Not surprisingly, it works perfectly and does its job extremely well. Ego limits and restricts our spiritual nature, by introducing the opposite of the perfection we are at birth and before. Our spiritual nature is love and has no knowledge or experience of anything else. The ego nature is fear.

Ego is formed by the information, thoughts, and emotions we learn and absorb through our five senses. This is done in two distinct modes. . .either consciously or *un*consciously. The human child is very close to his/her spiritual nature during the pregnancy and up to about a year or so after birth. At this time the deluge of information, some of which started even before birth, begins to cover the child's spiritual nature with the mask of the ego.

Self-awareness starts at about 18 months of age. Self-awareness is the recognition of the self to be separate from others, which, in turn, brings about the recognition of the world of duality. The world of duality is where perception starts. Perception is what allows humans to consciously decide how they are going to judge an emotion or event. Our judgment determines something to be right or wrong, good or bad, in human terms. This judgment then adds emotion and feelings to a belief already formed, which then becomes stronger.

Our personality starts to build before birth. (Remember the animal portion.) After birth, its growth picks up speed dramatically and becomes larger and denser, changing constantly. For the first six years of life children gather information about themselves, mostly unconsciously, like a sponge soaks up water. They absorb everything in their environments, and the information ends up in what we call the unconscious or subconscious mind. The child has little or no control over what information he or she is fed.

I describe *conscious* mind as working or deliberate thought. You are fully aware of what you are thinking and what it means to you at that moment (your perception). Conscious thought is mindful thinking, being in the moment. Being conscious is full awareness of your environment. Conscious thought is a choice made with purpose. We will eventually be discussing how important it is to be creating in your conscious thought. . .in other words, being ever mindful of what you want to create as your experience.

Unconscious mind is the part of the mind that accumulates information, sometimes without conscious thought. It is the storehouse of all past memories and thoughts. As a child, information is processed, having come from all the child's experience, as well as judgments or perceptions of that experience. In the beginning the child does not know what the information means or what the feelings and emotion behind it mean. Since a child cannot communicate well for the first two or three years, this is information fed in without the child's conscious awareness. All this information is used to develop beliefs, whether they are based on truth, or not.

Ego is fear-based. In our present society an excessive amount of information received daily is fear-oriented. A child's life is full of "watch out," "be careful," "you're going to get hurt," "why are you so stupid," "don't," and "you can't do that." You have, I'm sure, heard that "children have big ears." Well, it is a fact. Children pick up everything they hear around them. It stands to reason that they may not really understand everything they hear. Because of that misunderstanding, their perceptions can be distorted, and they carry those misperceptions on into their lives. They form beliefs about themselves and others, as well as the world, that are just plain mistaken.

Some examples of messages that could be heard and stored in the unconscious for future reference: "We never have enough money," "It's so hard to just get the bills paid," "Don't listen to anyone over 30. They don't know anything," or "This country is going downhill." "That kid will never amount to anything" is a comment that causes great harm to children in later life, even if unintentional. Even a seemingly innocent statement like "She just has trouble with math." can cause a child to always believe in having that trouble. These negative statements and resultant misunderstandings usually get filed under fear, unlovability, unworthiness, undeserving, or lack of belief in oneself.

These examples are a "mere drop in the bucket" of what can possibly be included in the development of a child's ego, the self-awareness portion of his/her personality. Children absorb everything they see, hear, smell, taste, and feel. "By the age of five, we have learned everything we need to know," a common expression and very close to the truth. After age 6 most of the information we receive only reinforces, for the most part, the belief systems we have formed in early childhood.

Because we really knew no better, each of us, as we grew to adulthood, took in most information from an outside source. We accepted it to be truth and have formed our individual belief systems. And, oh, how much of it has been incorrect. We didn't question authority, most of the time, and we assumed they (whoever they were) knew what they were talking about.

The ego mask covering our spiritual selves becomes very thick over a lifetime. The ego, by its nature, is negative. With a little introspection, it is easy for all of us to recognize that we hold a number of negative beliefs, which, in turn, create much negative thinking and judgment. The information that entered your consciousness, and the perception of that information, is what you became in later life. Your habitual thinking patterns are based on your beliefs. Your ego has tried to tell you that this is *who you are*, with all your misconceptions. But *you are not your ego*.

We now know that the human ego is formed with information received by our consciousness, starting before birth and continuing until death. Much of the information is negative, and most comes from other people's belief systems. This information is what makes us act the way we do, mostly automatically, without conscious thought.

The ego cannot be deleted, but it can be loved and nurtured. Its power can be used to serve your best interests. If your life is not what you want it to be, you must eliminate, diminish, or set aside the fear-based beliefs and the negative thoughts, emotions, and judgments associated with them. Then, your thoughts can begin to serve that which is in your highest and best good. Even a very traumatic negative event can be turned into a positive one, just by changing the thought about it and releasing the emotion. How you perceive an event is a choice. You do not have to be a victim.

You have complete control over your thought process. You can choose how information is cataloged and stored in your mind. New attitudes can be formed. You can have new beliefs about yourself. Best of all, you will discover who you really are and create for yourself the life you have always wanted. You can begin to learn how to listen only to that part of yourself that is God, your true wisdom.

Chapter 9

Human Nature
Spiritual Or Super-Ego

Man's total nature is a combination of the animal, ego, and spirit. This combination is what makes humans human, different from all others in the animal, plant, and mineral kingdoms. Although the three aspects of man's nature can be discussed separately, they are in fact one, intertwined like the web of a spider.

Our spiritual nature is our soul, which is God. The soul is located in every one of the trillions of cells in our bodies. It is the very essence of each cell. There is no place within us that soul is not present. It is the energy by which our body runs. When it leaves, the physical life ends.

Our spiritual nature comes from that which is perfect, God's Spirit. Spirit, by itself, because of its perfection, could not have allowed us to experience all the facets (the duality) of being a human being, which was God's original idea. If we had remembered who we really were, all would have been perfection on the earth. But God would also not have had the experience He desired. As God, living in human form, we would not have had the duality from which we make choices.

As discussed in Chapter 4, before the arrival of the soul,

humanoids had developed as an animal. When soul arrived, it gave us the awareness that we were different from all other forms. We became *self-aware*, and we learned quickly that we had some control over our environment, which no other species did have. The self-awareness provided by soul was the beginning of ego and the beginning of human personality.

Again, our spiritual nature is God. God is Mind. Our spiritual nature is Mind, God's Mind, and it is what gives us the ability to think. There are no separate minds, one for you, one for me. All mind is God's Mind. Thought, our use of the Mind, is God's communication system. God communicates with us through our minds, through our thoughts. Thought is the energy, power, or force that brings about the activity of Mind for manifestation (creation). We are the only ones in all the kingdoms that are capable of conscious thought and intentional creation, and it is due to our spiritual nature alone.

All ideas come from God. In the same way He communicates with us, through Mind, we also communicate with him. Because we are One with God, we are always communicating. Most of us, however, have led our lives totally unaware of this. When we receive ideas from God (and they *initially* can *only* be good), we do with them (using our egos) what we will. We are given free choice, and sometimes we make less-than-ideal choices.

Our thought process, the mechanism of this communication between God and our soul, is what creates our experience. By *consciously* entering into this place of Spirit, this place of Union, we have access to all that is within God's Mind, Universal Consciousness, which is *everything*. This doesn't just happen, because we logically *think* it to be a good plan of action. In order to access what is beyond our conscious memory, and really communicate with God, we have to *believe* it to be possible and *allow* it to happen. This cooperative use of Mind gives us, literally, ***unlimited possibilities***. Techniques to facilitate this communication will be discussed in a later chapter.

Each individual's consciousness is the sum total of all that has happened to him/her as a single human individual. This means all of our individual history, our choices, information, memories, emotions, thoughts, events, and all of our beliefs.

Let's take a look at how this mind connection works. Think of Universal Consciousness as a giant library and your individual consciousness is a book on a shelf. (It can also be imagined as a giant computer and your consciousness is stored as digital data in a folder with your name on it). This library has an unimaginable number of individual books. As we use our minds, we access the library every millisecond of every day, using a universal *indestructible* energy connection. Each time you need an idea, thought, or other information, you access it from your book. You can also access any information stored in the *whole* of Universal Consciousness. (That would be what those with developed psychic abilities would do.) For example, if you are looking for an anger thought, because your boss said something unpleasant, it will automatically come from your mind's past historical input. Your mind accesses old, stored anger thoughts. Scientists call this storage unit the subconscious mind.

Let's say you are trying to develop some new gadget or a new computer application. Having formed a desire in your mind and because of the energy of your thought process, a relevant idea comes from Universal Consciousness knowledge files. These files are where all ideas originate, including all the ideas that created the airplane, electric lights, steamboats, automobiles, atomic bombs, rockets, computers, i-phones, and everything else. All ideas relating to business, sports, economics, government, and anything you can imagine, comes from God's Universal Mind to our individual minds. They do not originate in our brain. These thoughts are *energy*, and the thought transfer happens so seamlessly and so quickly that it appears the information is stored in our brain. Universal Consciousness is so well-designed (God's device for creating) that the super-sized information storage system is a virtual reality within each one of us, as though we were one with it, which we are.

Knowledge of all that has ever happened (as well as all possibilities of the future) are stored in, and retrieved from, Universal Consciousness, or God Mind. The brain is an instantaneous retrieval mechanism, processing the thoughts, ideas, memories, emotions, and beliefs, which make up each individual personality. This all happens at the speed of thought, which is to say, instantly.

Without our connection to God's Mind we would not have an ego. We would not be able to reason or create. We would be animals. Our spiritual nature is our soul. The soul, because it is God, is not capable of giving us negative thoughts or feelings. The soul is very quiet, hardly ever speaks above a whisper, but speaks continually from within. The soul or spirit nature of man never sleeps and dwells as pure energy in every cell of our body. This energy is our built-in wireless device, used to communicate with God's Mind, Universal Consciousness. This wireless communication gives man extraordinary access to all that God is. We have direct access to unlimited power, unlimited wisdom and knowledge, and all unconditional love. Our soul knows this. It's our ego that fails to realize how we are connected to this Source.

When we die, our physical body and our human personality disappear. Our spirit returns to the realm of Spirit, to God, and all the information about us as a human is stored forever in Universal

Consciousness. Only Universal Mind has the intelligence that allows the universe and human life to function on the grand and glorious level that it does. Remember, we are not a human body looking for God. He is where we are. We are God in a human body.

Chapter 10
You Are Perfect

This is the point where we once again talk about who you *really are*, just in case you forgot for a moment (again). You are God. The *real* you, the God You, not the ego you, is the subject at hand.

Remember God's original idea? His idea, and everything He created, was manifested, or put in place, specifically so He could experience Himself in perfect human form. Would God expect to experience perfection in human form if it weren't possible? No! That would mean He could make a mistake. As a human, can you expect it to be possible to experience perfection? Yes! Is that at some time in the future when you have died and gone to an after-life? No. We are talking about *right now*. . .on this earth, just as it is and just as you are now, warts and all.

What is perfection, you ask? Or, at least, I hope you ask? You see examples of perfection continually. If you are reading this before the fire, and the snow is coming down hard, get up and look outside. Focus on one snow flake. That is perfection, for the snow flake is doing exactly what it was created to do, being itself. It is performing its creative purpose, which is perfection.

Another example is an apple seed. The seed is planted. It pursues its creative purpose and becomes an apple tree. It matters not what the tree looks like or where it is located. The seed performed its purpose to perfection. It gave forth fruit, becoming what its very nature said it was, an apple tree.

What do snow flakes and apple trees have to do with human beings? Snowflakes and trees are God, in snowflake and tree forms. You are God in human form. You and I, the tree, and the snowflake are all carriers of the energy which is God. All things have their parts to play in the game called life. That which you really are is perfect, this very instant. The energy of your soul is located in every cell of your body and is perfect. . . perfect here and perfect now.

You are perfection. How could it be any other way? You are God. You have expressed your God-Self many, many times over your lifetime. I'm sure of it. It may have lasted for seconds, minutes, or hours; but, none-the-less, you have attained perfection at some time. You have experienced and expressed *Yourself as God* every time you are *being* the perfection that is already in you, waiting to come forth. A simple example: Your child is distressed. You hold your child closely on your lap, comforting her and telling her how much you love her. You tell her that all is well (or similar verbiage). *You are being your God-Self* in those moments. Simple, isn't it? You are manifesting a situation that brings forth your God-Self, rather than your ego self, at that moment. You *intended* to be your God-Self and did what God would do. . .give love and comfort. You were being God at the same time as you were being your human self. That is God experiencing Himself in perfect human form. (See? God wouldn't expect something that isn't possible, and you have already proven it to be possible.) *THAT IS WHY YOU ARE HERE.* And your goal is to not only *do* that but to *be* that, every moment.

Contemplate the idea of what you are. Everything God is or has, you are and have. God *is* love, joy, kindness, compassion, selflessness, honesty, charity, peace, and more. And all of these equal happiness, which is the natural state of the human being. I'm sure you get the point. Each time you express who you *already innately* are, you are perfection in that moment. You are fulfilling your creative purpose. You are *being* God in perfect human form.

I hope you can now easily see that you are already perfect; and you have, at times, allowed that perfection to come forth, from your God-Self.

Chapter 11
Creation Process
Present Experience

You have now come to the point of understanding who and what you are, and why you are here. Right?

But, WOW! Where does all that understanding get you?

It gets you to just where you need to be. Where you are is totally and completely perfect. It's the place where change can come about, if desired. And we all have things we would like to change about our lives.

Since you made a choice to come into this physical realm to experience life, then some logical questions might be, "Shouldn't it be better than this? Why am I doing this in this particular way? Why does my life seem to be unfairly difficult? Can it be changed?" And the most pertinent question would be, "If I am God, then what's going on?"

The most simple answer to that last question is this: *You simply forgot.* And no one taught you what it was really all about. But, that forgetting is the simple reason for all that is going on with you now. You can fix it, however, if you want to. It will take practice, and it will take faith and belief, but *you can fix it*. You can create miracles in your life, little ones and big ones. We all can. We just have to believe it possible. We are all Holy Ones.

The material things you possess, all relationships you now have, all your present situations, together with all the beliefs you hold, have *all* been created by you, either *consciously* or *unconsciously*. You have some situations, relationships, and physical possessions that serve you well. You are happy with those.

At the same time, you might have situations, relationships, and both physical and mental stuff that displease you. These feelings of displeasure can be looked at as a positive. Your spiritual nature within is telling you that the negative situations you are thinking about are not in your best interest. This is your opportunity to choose to change the negative act or way of thinking to a positive, loving action. The Spirit/Soul is always peaceful and quiet, but not silent. It is consistent, persistent, and has infinite patience and love. This is the God within, and your true nature cannot be stilled.

Whatever your present physical, emotional, or mental experience might be, it can be changed for the better. Having a life of greatness, full to over-flowing with every type of imaginable abundance, is your Divine right.

You must, however, first believe that any change is possible. Then you must *choose* the physical or mental state you desire, in order to create it. Next, use *deliberate creation*, as God did, to attain it. This creation process has been consciously used by countless numbers of people before you to create new states of being for themselves. You can create the life you want, regardless of what is going on in the environment around you. Lest you forget, you are God.

If you have chosen to make changes in some part of your life, whether they are physical or mental changes, you are going to have to change your beliefs and your thought process. Your habitual thoughts (those you think over and over again) are brought about by what you believe to be true, whether it is true or not. And some of those beliefs were formed by you, more or less by default. Beliefs of your family, friends, community, etc. you took to be yours, just because you assumed them to be true. Well, you have to take responsibility for any of them that are not serving you well now. You cannot change the past, so that is not your concern and certainly not something you should feel guilty about. The only moment that counts is the present one.

Included in the process of becoming more self-aware is the *conscious* awareness of what your beliefs actually are. Like most of us, you probably take most of them very much for granted. You might have to address and question them, one by one, and determine if there might be untruths you have allowed yourself to hold onto. No one can undertake this process for you. You also have to take responsibility for that fact. The reason you do not already have the things you desire may very well be because of your false beliefs. Those false beliefs could be about yourself, others, situations, misunderstandings, etc. The list could be very long. Your thoughts and actions reflect those beliefs back into your experience, just like a mirror. Look closely at that mirror.

As humans we all create, all the time, just as God created the universe. God created everything using the deliberate creation process, which is manifesting with *conscious thought (energy)*. Although this may sound daunting, you are using a creation process as we speak, whether you realize it or not. That's just the way our universe operates. The question is. . .what creation process are you using, to what extent is it being used, and is the one you are using serving your highest and best good? Are you using conscious thought, or are you creating out of subconscious beliefs that aren't even true? Everything in your life has been created by you, *no one else*, not your parents, your spouse, your boss, no one. But this present moment is all you have to work with, and you do have the creative power within you to change anything about your life that you no longer wish to have as a part of your experience. Contemplate that for a few moments. . .*you are sooooooo powerful*!

You will find that if you want to change anything physical, emotional, or mental, you will be working with what you have perceived to be negative. Do not let this bother you. You are not alone. Every one of us has a huge storehouse of negative thoughts and beliefs. Remember, no guilt about the past! You are working toward improving your present and your future. You have power, wisdom, and love at your disposal to change whatever it is about yourself or your situation that you find displeasing. You need only choose to do so and then act. However, always keep in mind that you cannot change another. Those around you will have to feel a need to make their own changes. What you can change is your reaction to others. If what you are feeling is negative, then you will be working on changing that negative feeling into something that is more to your liking, more beneficial for you.

Let's say, for example, you do not like your present job. If you have a negative self-image or self-worth issue, it might be difficult for you to believe (that word again) that you can just go get a new job, especially if you believe (there it is again!) we are living in hard times. Without a new job, some of the things you would like to manifest feel a thousand miles away and impossible to achieve. So what is called for is major belief and thought changes.

Any negative beliefs about yourself were probably given to you by other human beings, at least originally. By *believing* another's negative judgment about you, you have affirmed it to be true, even if it isn't. Further, you have fed this belief by *habitually* thinking it and forcing it into the subconscious level. These beliefs can be changed, however, employing various thought techniques. You can eliminate the negative beliefs, change your thoughts and emotions, and create a whole new you.

I realize that many of your present beliefs may be unknown to you. I understand they can be completely hidden from view by the mask of the ego. I have gone through the same processes that I will be discussing here, and I continue to go through them every day. I can also say I have found emotions and negativity in myself that I did not know I had, nor did I know the reason for them. I have changed some completely and am still working on others. I know there are some I have yet to find. It is interesting to note that once you find one, you will find others.

We are very complex beings, and the path to self-discovery is not a one-day trip. Beliefs and thoughts go hand-in-hand. When you change one, another can change almost automatically. Every individual has to do the work on his/her own. I am going to give you some tools to help you accomplish exactly that. This is the moment!

Chapter 12

Thought

Thought is consciousness in action, pure energy, that which brings the activity of the mind into manifestation.

Man does not think as a *separate* entity from God. That would be impossible, in that we are God, and there is only one Mind. It can be said that *only* God thinks. It can also be said, "as God, we think." There is a very well-known quote by philosopher René Descartes (1596-1650): "I think; therefore, I am." This statement, his most well-known, has been cussed and discussed for centuries. Descartes spoke in the context that he knew he existed, because he could think. I think of it as: I think because I am God. Inclusive in the idea that God lives in us, through us, and as us, would be the necessity that God thinks through us. Thought comes from mind, and, again, there is only one Mind.

We came into this physical life, knowing innately that we have the power to create. That part of us that is God created the universe, and *as* God *we knew it*. Within our being we know we have power. But. . .very early on, in childhood, the big world out there quickly started to give us messages that we weren't powerful, that we couldn't necessarily do what we wanted to do or have what we wanted to have. And, unfortunately, we believed them (each to his/her own degree). But, nonetheless, we were bombarded with these messages. We still are! (Watched any TV lately?) And we bought into it. We bought into how hard life is, how easy it is to become a victim, how we are susceptible to so many diseases, how we aren't good-looking enough. Fear! Fear! Fear! We gave away our power, so to speak.

There are many experts out there who might have many different names for this "hypnotized" part of our mind. I rather think "ego mind" fits the bill.

Many have come to believe, to a great extent, that this is "just the way it is--reality." And believing in this *false* reality is what has caused us to seem to separate ourselves from God, even though that is impossible. There is only one Mind, not God's Mind *and* our mind. But this ego mind makes us think we have a separate mind. Sometimes we even go so far as to say we have no control over it. (We will be dealing with that notion later.)

This ego mind has a ***great deal*** of influence over our thought process. We unconsciously allow ourselves to store all sorts of negative misinformation in our subconscious, as if it were all true. We sometimes aren't too picky about what goes in there. If we don't choose to think ***consciously, on purpose,*** the old, negative, possibly untrue beliefs come forward and automatically influence what we think, what we feel, and therefore what we manifest. This is creating by default.

How we feel is the effect of how we think. We can readily observe how powerful thought is in our experience. We merely have to observe how we are feeling at any given moment. If we aren't feeling good, and we make a conscious effort to change our thinking to that which does make us feel good, it is obvious how our feeling is the effect of our thought (cause). It has been said in some very great books that when we came into this physical life we gave ourselves a way to determine when we were thinking thoughts that did not resonate with our soul. It is rather simple, really. We feel bad.

Thought is magnified in power when more than one of us has the same thought, at the same time, focused on the same result. The more people involved, the higher degree of power. There are innumerable instances of the positive effects of group prayer. However, the opposite mentality would be evident in such events as Hitler's Germany. Hitler's ability to influence so many people would be an exaggerated example of a negative group mentality.

The way you think is who you are. At any given moment, you are who you choose to be. Yes, you are *choosing* to be patient or impatient. To say, "I can't help it." is an untruth. This simply means you *can* alter your life, and everything about it, by the way you think. Universal Consciousness, along with and the Law of Creation, will give you whatever you choose.

God loves unconditionally and impersonally, but the law of creation works both for the positive and for the negative. This may be hard to grasp, but if it worked any other way, it would defeat the purpose of God's original idea, which included freedom of choice. To manage your thought is to manage your life. How you think forms your beliefs and attaches emotion to these beliefs. When you practice the same thought, either positive or negative, long enough, the beliefs you form then build habits. Habits manifest in the physical, showing up as your reaction to any given circumstance.

You use thought for every step of creation. It is the tool you use for self-examination, to determine what you want to change. You use it to form a picture of what that change would look like. And you then use it to execute the change, by deciding what steps are necessary. Thought is with you 24/7, so why not use it *consciously* to improve your life?

God is power, wisdom, and love and gives you thoughts and

ideas to deliberately create anything you want. Because God is love, the ideas He gives you can *only* be those that are good. It is what you do with them that creates your experience.

A rather generic example would be: God gives you the idea that you want more money in your life. By using God Mind and God's aspects, which are all positive (love, kindness, patience, etc.), you can mindfully search for ways that you can bring more affluence to yourself, by focusing on how you can do that (more education or training), by *knowing* that you can do it, and by always keeping the picture in your mind of what you *want*, rather than what you *don't want*. Or, by using your fear-based ego mind, you can pervert the idea of making more money by stealing it from someone else. The God-given idea was perfect in the first place. With your free choice you may do with it what you will.

When you *feel* badly about a situation, act, or thought, this is your God-Self reminding you that what you are thinking and doing is not in your highest and best interest. The feeling (sometime called gut feeling or intuition) is the way your spirit nature always communicates with you in every situation. You can always know how well you are doing on your spiritual path by the way you *feel* at that given moment. God and your individual God-Self express only that which is for your good.

What makes you think you can't be what you want to be or have what you want? What are all the arguments and excuses your ego gives you to keep you from your desire? Are they judgment statements like these? You're too short, too old, too young, too addicted. You're uneducated or too set in your ways.

These are low-energy thoughts retrieved from your subconscious mind. They disrupt your energy and are a cause of the bad feelings you experience within yourself. These types of thoughts are always based on negative false beliefs and emotions about yourself. When negative thought is released and replaced with positive thought, your energy increases and the disruptions disappear. With higher positive loving energy your happiness and joy return. All positive, loving thoughts are much more powerful.

Becoming aware of the role thought plays in the law of creation is, obviously, a vital aspect of this entire discussion. Knowing who you are and the power you have is the beginning. Acknowledging your responsibility for your thought process is the next required step. Then, with practice, you are free to create anything you want to have or to be. Have fun! Feel the joy! And give thanks for *ALL YOU ARE!*

Science and Thought

Positive thought given to Universal Consciousness brings about positive ideas and information in return. This is the law of "like attracts like," and this has been demonstrated over and over in human experience. When you add emotion to thought, it has been shown to increase the thought's effectiveness and strength. Positive thought can change the chemicals in the brain and influence the DNA. Both individual thought and group thought have been proven to change people's health, cure disease and even reduce the crime rate over extended periods of time. Thought can move objects, and some people's thoughts can attach to distant events and places with scientific precision. All this, too, has been demonstrated in human experience and scientific studies.

We also have scientific research that shows higher activity and energy in the brain when positive thought is present, and lower energy readings when negative thought is held. In actual electrical measurement tests, positive thought can raise the body's vibration rate by 10 to 15 MHz. Negative thoughts can lower frequency by

12-15 MHz. This is just a small example of the potential possibilities your thoughts, emotions, and feelings contain.

The fact that thought can raise the body's frequency rate or lower it says that the way you think can make both physical body changes and mental changes. For example, the healthy human body measures somewhere between 62-72 MHz. If your frequency level drops to around 58 MHz, conditions like colds and flu appear. At lower levels, around 42 MHz, major disease can be found. Notice that the difference between a low healthy reading of 62 MHz and cold and flu levels is only 4 MHz, and the difference to the disease level is only 20 MHz. It is not hard to see how eliminating negative emotions and beliefs and adding positive beliefs and thoughts, even a little, could make dramatic changes in a person's life. If this program was directed and delivered using deliberate positive thoughts within a plan and done correctly; can you see the possibilities?

Everything everywhere has a frequency, a vibration level. What you desire has its own unique frequency level, which is already in Universal Consciousness. If you will remember Einstein's quote (in Chapter 4), when your frequency matches that of what you seek, it must manifest. This is physics, pure and simple. The catch, of course, is that it is not practical to measure each human's vibration level, because it changes day-to-day. Measuring the vibration level of what each person is trying to create is not only impractical but, at the moment, impossible. (One should never say "impossible" when talking about God powers, so let's say "working on it.")

Scientific testing has shown that all thought changes the chemistry and size of the brain, in one way or another. The chemistry change can then change DNA by turning off or turning on the switches in the DNA, which controls cell function. It has been determined that negative thoughts, which cause negative emotions, may be responsible, at least in part, for causing the precursors of disease, such as inflammation. Negative thoughts and emotions cause stress, which has been found to be a major cause of illnesses such as heart disease, stroke, cancer, and depression. In brain scan research, people who focus on negative aspects of themselves or think about a negative interpretation of life, generate a destructive neurochemical reaction, which, over time, can cause damaging changes to their brain. That's the bad news.

The good news is it can *all* be reversed with positive thoughts and actions. *Anything can be changed!* Positive thought can reverse disease and change any human fear to love. Positive thought, which is prayer (as all thought is prayer), can release negativity and turn stress to peace, even when everything seems to be falling to pieces.

Here is something else about thought. Scientific research done by Andrew Newberg, M.D. has shown that positive religious and spiritual contemplation (thought) changes the brain; because it strengthens a unique neural circuit that specifically enhances social awareness and empathy, while subduing destructive feelings and emotions. *Fear-based* religious and spiritual thought causes an opposite and negative effect, which can actually damage the brain. Now there's a notion! Thought changes the brain in physical ways.

Chapter 13
Believe In Yourself

I harp on believing in yourself quite a bit, as you have probably noticed. One of the reasons people have a hard time with *deliberate* creation is because they do not realize or believe in the innate power they have. For the most part, churches and religion certainly do not teach that the human being has this power because of his divinity. They, in fact, teach just the opposite. Most of their adherents are taught to believe that only a few holy people over the millennia have had this power.

In order to create what you want, you must believe in *yourself*, in *your* power and ability to create deliberately. It is not a requirement that you believe this 100%; that will come later. You, in fact, don't even *have* to believe in God. You do not *have* to believe that you are God. You do not *have* to believe in anything other than *yourself* to get the same practical experience of manifesting what you want. I, however, simply believe there is a Universal Law of God that brings about *all* creation, *all* that is seen and unseen. That Law has always worked for you, despite whether you believe in it or not. And it will always work.

Whatever you choose to believe as to how creation comes about, whether it is according to God's Law or something else, you none-the-less *must* believe that what you want is possible to attain. Of course the opposite has to be true, also. If you believe that something you want is impossible, it will be impossible (*for you*--perhaps not for someone else). The higher your level of belief, the quicker your desire can come about. If you believe that what you want is possible to achieve in some way, shape, or form, this is all Universal Consciousness needs to begin its creation process. By believing in your ability to create exactly and purposefully what you desire, you can change your life.

With Universal Consciousness you have limitless potential. You have the ability to create anything you can imagine. You have already created many emotions, beliefs, relationships, and material possessions in your life. You have formed judgments that some are good and some not so good. Areas of your life that are now to your liking have been created from the positive belief you have formed about yourself. Every positive item you will be asked to list in Chapter 16 indicates that belief, whether it was formed consciously or *un*consciously.

All of us have, to some degree, doubts and fears about ourselves and just do not believe that we are as good as we actually are. Think consciously that you are God; you are a divine being just waiting to blossom. You are equal to any other human on the planet. Thought is the single most powerful force on earth. Use your powerful thought process to think of yourself as great. Think this without let-up. Through the power of God's creative process, the belief you have in yourself will increase significantly.

Believing in yourself is an *inside* job. Your truth and your power are within. There is nothing outside of you that is necessary for you to begin your creation process. Don't impede your progress by creating a dependence on others to reinforce your positive beliefs. It is only *your* belief in yourself that counts. Reinforcement from others can add to your belief, to a degree, but it is your work for yourself that will be the ultimate positive reinforcement. You must become dependent on what you think about yourself. We all have to do that.

What you presently think and believe is who you are now and is the reason for what you have now. Your believing makes it so. Everything that is presently you, your body, your health, your personality, your environment, your world, you created with your thought. What you believe and how you think from this minute forward is what your future life will be.

Let no other human being restrain you from your dreams and desires. Any negative belief can be changed, and any positive belief can be strengthened. Merely choose to do so. You have already created many positive things in your life, such as relationships, homes, jobs, etc. You attracted these things to yourself because you believed them to be possible. Let *ALL* things be possible.

Once again, you are God. As God, you can do anything. Just start. Get a bracelet that says "BELIEVE." Wear it all the time. Put signs up all over your home that says, "BELIEVE." Tell yourself over and over, "I Am God. I can do this." And continually use various positive *I AM* phrases. . ."I am _____." Use words like brilliant, great, healthy, happy, an artist, a writer, a mechanic, a lover, and any other words you can think of that you want to make your reality. Say them over and over. Look in a mirror and boldly say them to yourself, eye-to-eye. Say them out loud; yell them if you wish. Say them even if you have trouble believing it for now. Remember, practice makes perfect. Keep in mind how much of the negative stuff you have to *un-do*. (Don't get bogged down with any guilt about what has to be un-done, because *anything* can be un-done.) Remember *all thought*, whether it is positive or negative, *is prayer*.

If saying these positive words out loud especially bothers you,

you can rest assured you have a negative belief about yourself that needs to be worked on and released. (We will discuss this release process in Chapter 17.) If you were to say, for example, "I am a great writer" and get that queasy, upset, funny feeling in your stomach, that comes from a negative belief about yourself. This is your mind trying to get your attention.

When you do this positive thought work, Universal Consciousness begins the creation process. Not only will you raise your own self-esteem and belief, God will give you ideas and a direction in which to go. You will be amazed at how opportunities present themselves, especially if you look for them.

Chapter 14

Consciousness

Our Mind

As I have said, our mind is a part of God Mind, the total Universal Mind. Our conscious mind, as I will be discussing it, is our *individual mind*, which is rather like the tree is a part of the forest.

Many people have tried to explain how our minds work. Many labels have been attached to consciousness. For the rest of our time together here, I am going to use only two labels. These two are the *conscious* and the *subconscious*.

The individual *conscious* mind refers to our act of purposeful thinking, mindfulness, or awareness. Our conscious mind is equipped with decision, discrimination, and will. It has self-choice.

The *subconscious* mind is the part that is beneath awareness, so to speak, and is what causes an automatic response to whatever the conscious mind has taken in. The only part of the subconscious mind we are going to deal with is the storage area, the place where our beliefs and emotions are recorded. It accepts information from the conscious and creates emotions based on the information stored.

With the creative power of our thought, we have control over both of these areas. Using our thought in conjunction with creative tools, we can, through use of our conscious mind, manipulate the subconscious and replace falsehood with truth, negative with positive. The subconscious doesn't care. You have, in the past, fed in a lot of junk. It wasn't picky about what it accepted as truth. Let's clean it up!

All of us have good things going on in our lives. These positive aspects of our life will be used as building blocks when we review our present thoughts and feelings (coming up in Chapter 16). The beliefs and emotions we are concerned about, however, are the negative ones. These are already imbedded in our subconscious mind, and it is these we must first deal with in order to make the creation process simpler. If we can eliminate the use by our subconscious minds of negative emotions and beliefs, just that alone would improve our lives greatly. And that is what we are going to do.

Whenever our five senses assimilate some occurrence, our conscious mind registers the information and has the ability to take control, by producing a mindful reaction. Or, it can default to the subconscious mind, which accesses previously-held beliefs about that particular type of occurrence and sends back an automatic reaction. Such occurrences could be events, something heard, something seen, even something tasted, smelled, or touched. If we don't stop and make a conscious, mindful decision about what our reaction will be, the subconscious will take over and use its information, based on previous experience, and send it back to the conscious, resulting in either a positive or a negative reaction. This happens so quickly, we are not aware of it. This defaulting to the subconscious can be quite alright, if the right information is stored there. We want it to be positive. Then, when we do default, the reactions will be positive. We all have the ability to eventually fill our subconscious with so much positive information, overwriting all the negative, that we cease to react to the world around us with any negativity. What a worthy goal!

Negativity in the subconscious can cause a great deal of trouble and harm. Here is an example from my own experience. I became aware of the fact that I had a negative re-action every time my wife questioned something I was doing or saying. I took the comment as criticism, even when it was not, which was the case most of the time. By using the tools I will share later, I found that I had a false belief that I was not worthy, which resulted in the feeling that I had to be right all the time in order to prove my worthiness. (That's what the need to be right is all about.) There were also other emotions attached to this particular belief, such as embarrassment, resentment, and anger. When this particular situation arose, I would react automatically with some degree of irritation or anger. If it escalated, it could end up in an argument. This is not something I wanted to continue. Using the creative process of thought, emotional release, meditation, and affirmations, I have reduced this reaction to a place where, if it arises, I can now stop the negative reaction from happening. Soon it will not even show up, because it has been replaced with a positive belief that, no matter what is said, I have a deeper belief in myself. My God-Self inherently has no need to prove Its worthiness.

The subconscious mind can be changed, because it has no will of its own. It does what it is told, regardless of the consequences. This is why the way you think, pray, affirm, speak, or write is so important. When correctly done in a positive communication, the law of "like attracts like" takes over; and you build a positive-based subconscious mind, rather than negative-based. When your subconscious mind is programmed with positive beliefs in yourself, reinforced with positive emotions, success in all facets of your life becomes much easier to accomplish.

This is the way God designed man for his role as God, experiencing in human form. We have a beautiful mind. It is the God Mind. We have been given free choice to use it as we will. If we have misused the power of this mind, we need to know how we did that, how we can change that by re-writing the script, and how to start staging our play (life) with its new script.

Chapter 15
Creating Positive Experience

God's creative process, as outlined in Chapter 4, seems to be simple in the telling; but I have found that it is a little harder as a human in the accomplishing. It is harder because we have a built-in resistance system called the ego, and the ego (as well as the world out there) has told us we don't have the power. The process of creating a positive life experience can be learned and mastered, however, using the tools the Creator has provided for us by design. Thoughts, words, and actions are the agents of creation. Thought is the foundation of it all. It is the very essence of the whole process, at every step along the way to manifestation.

Intentional creation usually begins with a feeling you get that you want something better, or dissatisfaction with the status quo. This feeling is from God. Your God-Self *always, always* wants your life to be better and more abundant in every way, and It consistently and quietly directs you toward the role of who you really are. If you are receptive to Its direction, a positive *idea* will form in your mind. Initially, it might just be a subtle "I could. . . . ." As you focus on this idea, more ideas will come, and *desire* will begin to build. You will see more possibilities inherent in your desire. Your thought is now tapping into Universal Consciousness, or God Mind; and everything contained therein is yours to use, as you choose. You will then be able to purposefully and intentionally begin to create your desire. (Later, we will be showing you some tools that can help you to more quickly and powerfully manifest.)

You have now given thought to an idea, and have reached the point of desire. Again, using your thoughts, you begin to form *pictures* in your mind of what you want. We think in pictures; this is automatic. Focus on those pictures, remembering to abstain from forming pictures of what you *don't want*. Negative input dilutes the power of your visualization. Embellish your pictures. . the more elaborate the better. Give your pictures details, making them vivid. Imagine what you will *feel* when you achieve what you desire. The stronger the feelings, the quicker the results.

Do you remember the discussion in Chapter 4 of God's speaking "the word" to bring forth his desire? Well, that is exactly what you should do to bring about yours. Using the same tool that God did, His Word, begin to *speak* your desire forth. Tell others, if they are receptive. (Don't let *anyone* discourage you.) Talking to someone else about your desire could lead to other people or situations that could help you. This is how God works to bring your desires forth. Be receptive. Listen for messages. Look for messages. They can come from anywhere. *Expect* to see what you want. (This is vital! We get what we expect!)

If it helps to increase the picture of success in your mind, write your ideas down. It's another way to express your word and to focus on what you want. Your excitement will increase, as well as your belief in yourself and your success.

An important aspect of speaking your desire forth, whether it is verbal or written, is to speak in the present. God has heard your request. Remember, all thought is prayer. It is *already* accomplished, waiting for you to bring it about in your experience. That may be hard for you to fathom, but have faith in it. Speak as if it already *is* in place. Express gratitude for it. You might feel uncomfortable doing this, at first, but keep at it. Pretend if you have to. It will come. Remember the Wright brothers? No one thought they could make a machine that would fly. But they spoke it, saw it in their minds, and believed it, until it came about, a most perfect example of intentional creation.

You have now created a great idea with your thoughts and your words. Next is an oh-so-important part of creation, the *doing*. You have to follow through with action. What you want will probably not just drop in your lap. You have to take action to manifest what you want, whether it's a belief change, a physical object, or a situation change. Although the power does exist to manifest simply with thought alone, most of us have not reached that spiritual evolvement yet. We have to do it the old-fashioned way. We have to roll up our sleeves and get to work. The doing might be all mental, or it might include hard physical labor. It all depends on the nature of the creation. Also, it might only involve you, or it might involve many others. (When I say "many others," I do not mean to imply trying to control others.) For humans at our stage of spiritual development, the doing part can be the most difficult to get a handle on. Some of us can manifest a particular outcome really well, and fail miserably at another. That's o.k. . we're all "works in process" of becoming what we want to be.

One of my goals is to help you make your life better and, at the same time, give you an inkling of who you really are and what powers of creation you have available to you. If this inspires you, maybe you will inspire others. We *all* gain; because, as God, we are *all one*.

I understand the above creation description is relatively simple. I have always believed in KIS (keep it simple). These simple steps, the knowledge that you are God, plus the tools we are going to talk about in the coming chapters, will give you what you need to create a life full of love, harmony, peace, and joy, if that is what you choose.

In Chapter 12 we discussed the vibration of thought. Everything in the universe has a vibration, things we see (money, lovers, jobs, homes) and things we don't see (thought, peace, safety, happiness). When trying to bring anything into our experience, we must match the vibration of our thought of it to the thing itself. This is called the Law of Attraction. Again, like attracts like. It's a simple concept, but it is vitally important to remember when trying to bring about a mental or physical change.

If we want to create new situations, behaviors, or physical accomplishments in our lives, we need to raise our vibration levels, until we match the vibration level of the accomplishment we are seeking. We do this by thinking only good things, positive and loving things. We may not know the vibration level of the things we are seeking, but we do have the knowledge, methods, and tools that allow us to raise our vibrations. We are also safe in the knowledge that people everywhere have done these same things before, by using these same methods and tools. The one thing we are sure of; we do not now have the condition we seek. Therefore, we need to make changes in order to create something different. Doing the same thing we are doing now will only continue to produce what we have now. It is not enough to simply abstain from negative thoughts. We must actively think positively. We must think, feel, and act differently. We, literally, must **be** someone else.

Think of a change you would like to bring about in your life. Now that you know the process of creation, you can begin to make the necessary changes in your thought process. It takes practice; and, hopefully, you are committed to that practice. You can take control and maintain control, until what you want appears. Universal Consciousness will know what you desire, and it has to fulfill your demand. It is the Law of Deliberate Creation.

CHAPTER 16
Self-Examination
The Starting Point

You have reached the point where you have declared that *something has to change*, and the time to make that change is *now*. Are you serious about this? Are you willing to put in some work? Because, dear one, it will take some work. This won't happen overnight, but you will notice changes rather soon if you put in some good, solid effort into it. Regardless of how big or how small the change you have in mind is, that change can be yours.

I am going to suggest some techniques here that are a little time-consuming in the beginning. This will take some thought work. At times this thought process may be a little painful, or maybe even quite painful. But, in the long run, aren't you worth it, if it helps you? I know you are worth it. Perhaps, you think that's easy for me to say, because I don't even know you. But, please be assured, we are all worth only the best in our lives, *all of us,* no matter what has happened in the past. You might believe you've committed the greatest of "sins," but sins are merely mistakes. (Yes, murder is a *mistake*, certainly with justifiable consequences.) You can start over, wherever you might be at this moment. This moment is the only one that counts, and it can be the start of your *"something big."*

What is it about your life you want to make better? What is it you want to change? What do you have negative feelings about? I have found that the whole process works better and easier, if first we turn our attention to reviewing where we are right now. This process will take awhile, if your aim is to find happiness. We all have an incredible amount of negativity lodged inside our subconscious mind. Unfortunately, that's just the way the world has worked at feeding us information. However, the world is not at fault. We have chosen our reactions to it, consciously or unconsciously.

Releasing it all is a time-consuming project. However, it is not difficult. For those people who stay with it, there are unlimited rewards waiting for you. The key is **persistence**. As you work at this process, you will feel better from day one; and your feeling of well-being will increase as you continue. Try to focus on these better feelings as you go along. The better your focus, the more those feelings will grow. *The better it gets, the better it gets.*

Letter to God

My first suggestion is to write a letter to God, telling Him exactly what you want your life to be from this point on. This letter will serve many functions. It will be immediately assimilated by Universal Consciousness, and ideas and information for creation will begin to flow back to you. A written document of any kind is a tool of creation I call "the word." Your writing will give you a clearer picture as to where it is you wish to go and what you want to change in your life.

This letter can cover physical, emotional, and mental changes. I suggest you concentrate heavily on how you want your life to look and be, from a *feeling* standpoint. What is happiness to you? What is love? How will you feel when your desire comes to be your experience? Write down your life dreams and desires, such as a new relationship, improvement of old ones, a different job or promotion, and those things you love to do, but are not now doing. This letter can and may be re-written often, if you stick with the process. Put in every detail you can think of. Go so far as describing colors, places, what things will look like, how you and/or others might act. This is putting in an order to the universe; so give it all you've got, so the universe can give you all it has, which is unlimited. Only you and God will ever see this, so reach for the stars!

Writing like this may be totally unfamiliar to you, but **PLEASE, PLEASE, PLEASE**, keep at it. If you feel clumsy, and even the slightest inadequate, keep at it. Remember, no one else has to see this and it is for your highest and best good.

*   *   *

Obviously, everyone wants real happiness. But we aren't necessarily taught what produces happiness. We tend to mistakenly believe that happiness will come about from something outside ourselves, when we have the right relationship, enough money, or the right circumstance in our life at the time. Unhappiness is, in fact, our *reaction* to those events of our lives, not *because* of them.

However, we don't necessarily know how to create this happiness in ourselves. This is primarily due to the resistance and limitations we *think* we have. Our negative beliefs, feelings, and emotions are the cause of doubts and fears about ourselves. With these removed, fashioning new beliefs and emotions will go much smoother. We will, literally, be working on getting rid of the old to make room for the new.

We are now going to set about finding as many negative beliefs, emotions, and feelings, which are causing our inability to always express or receive love and experience true happiness and joy. When you exaggerate the positive and eliminate the negative, you will find all you have left is love. And as I have said, love is what we are.

Suggestion #2 is to find these negative beliefs, emotions, and feelings. I suggest the old-fashioned, tried-and-true method, "The List." This is an old creative method taught by many teachers for many years, and it still works as well now as it has in the past. We will make two lists, one positive and one negative.

The Love List

The first is the **love** list. List what is good and positive about your life, things you are grateful for. Try to be as complete as possible. Include all the positive people in your life, jobs, hobbies, health, homes, material possessions. Focus on various aspects of your life to identify the emotions, feelings, and beliefs you have about them. Anything you can think of as good, list it. Have a good time with this list. We will use it again in the chapter on gratitude; and you will discover that you want to come back and add to it, as you release negativity. Check Appendix I for a list of some positive words to help you get started.

The Fear List

The next list is the *fear* list. This list is likely to be rather long, if you really put in the effort to identify all those things which displease you. This means *anything* negative, not just big things, like fear of flying. Check Appendix II for examples of negative emotions and false beliefs found in the majority of people. When looking at the words in the examples, concentrate on the feeling the word gives you; and write down everything that comes to mind. Search through all past relationships for anything negative you can think of. This is all relationships. Include family, friends, lovers, co-workers, former co-workers, and bosses. If you are the average person, you have had negative feelings, emotions, situations, slights, insults, put downs, and resentments. Your subconscious still contains every one of them. List all the jobs you didn't get that you wanted, every promotion you might not have gotten, every class you did badly in, every teacher you disliked, or anyone else you disliked.

Go back as far as you can to your teen years or earlier, if possible, especially if there was a traumatic event. Here comes the toughie. Put down every bad situation that has happened to you. Include any abuse of any kind, including sexual abuse, rape, any physical abuse from family, friends, or bullies, or any other crimes committed against you. Yes, the emotions buried from these events can be released. It may take some work, but it can be done. And, again, always remember that no one else has to see this list.

On your fear list include former spouses, former friends, anyone that jilted you, former lovers. Look hard at your siblings and parents, too. What are your prejudices? How do you feel about the world around you? Do you have some fear of human interaction, like sales, asking someone for a date, or talking to strangers? How do you feel when a friend, even in jest, makes an unflattering remark? What is your relationship with food? How do you feel about your body? How do you feel when your spouse breaks down crying?

This is not about finding fault, nor is it the blame game. You are simply claiming responsibility for *your reaction* to everything that has happened to you. In the present moment, you are not a victim, no matter what has happened in the past. You are now only a victim, so to speak, of your memories, and your emotional reactions. Those memories and emotional reactions are all that is causing you harm now, nothing or no one out there is presently at fault. You are finding feelings and beliefs that are buried in your subconscious and are holding you back. If you want things to change, if you want a better, happier life, keep working on this list.

Examine how you act under difficult situations. How do you feel when someone criticizes you or your work? Do you judge others? We all do, to some degree. Write down what and who you judge. This judgment thing is a biggie. Observe how easy it is for you to judge something said or done. . .even something as innocuous as a TV ad. One thing to keep in mind: when you see fault in others, it is usually a mirror of something in you. . .maybe something you aren't particularly aware of. These judgments definitely need to be added to the list.

You may be thinking by now that this fear list is never-ending. I've gone on and on, trying to give you ideas of where to look for all that negative stuff. The longer and more intensively you look, the longer the list can get. How many years has this been going on? Probably, the longer your life, the longer the list. Don't be intimidated. Know that by working on one negative emotion or belief and releasing it, more will undoubtedly be released at the same time. And, this doesn't all have to be accomplished this week, or this year, for that matter. Be patient, both with yourself and with the process!

In the past you have thought, that if someone or something would change in your life, all would be well. You have no power to change anyone else. You are only working on yourself here. You will have to leave others to their own choices, when it comes to change. We have started the process of doing just that. . .*FOR YOU*. Any change that comes about is *for* you, *by* you, and *in* you. How that change might affect others will be an added bonus.

These are secret lists you share only with God, if that is what you choose; and God never rats out. Write down all the negative feelings and beliefs that come to mind. Take as long as you need. You can sort them out later. You can also add to them, as new ones come to mind. You can subtract from them; and you will, as you release them from your subconscious. That is your ultimate goal. It sometimes only takes minutes to dissolve a negative feeling, and sometimes the toughies can take many tries. We will discuss the releasing process in the next chapter.

Write down all those things you really want changed and have seemed to be unable to change, so far. It is time to release them. The more you release, the more love and happiness you will find. Every time you release one thing, your capacity to love, your happiness, joy, and peace increase. You will be much more successful if you are honest with yourself. In fact, brutal honesty is best for you in the long run.

It should go without saying, but it doesn't, that you men have these same emotions buried down there. It's not just a "girl thing." Men like to think they don't have emotions. For the most part, they are certainly taught by our culture not to express them. So they get hidden. The resulting negative reactions could be affecting your relationships and the emotional responses you give out. The biggest complaint of women everywhere is that men do not understand women's emotions or how to respond to them. By releasing negative feelings and beliefs, those unwanted emotional responses can be reduced, if not removed altogether.

Here are some examples: If you become aware that your self-esteem is less than you like, and work on releasing the emotions involved, it will change many facets of your life, not just the one you might have been most concerned about. By getting rid of some anger, your job, your relationships, even your athletic ability could be improved. A reduction of the anger in you could affect everyone around you. When you change, others will automatically respond to your change.

As you get happier your outlook changes, and both your confidence and your belief in yourself will increase. I have seen it in my own life, and others as well. The higher your love and happiness levels go, the more you will *want* to work on it, and your positive feelings increase even more. It just spirals upward.

*   *   *

With your lists complete, at least for now, you have a place to start. Next, you can list them in order, or use any other method you wish to pick the ones to work on first. I can tell you from experience, the more you think about your lists, the more ideas and thoughts God will give you. If you can spend a little time each day, focusing on making changes, the rewards will be great. I advise keeping a small notebook handy, because thoughts and ideas often come at inconvenient times. Make notes to yourself, things you want to remember later.

I also suggest you keep everything you write, your lists, etc. Over time you are going to change. Later, reading these things can help you see those changes. You might be amazed that thoughts you have now are no longer appropriate for your life at a later time. There will be progress, if you work on it. That is a promise.

Chapter 17
Releasing Negative Beliefs
And Emotions

Any time you express love you are expressing and experiencing God. All positive feelings are some form of love. All negative feelings, even the lesser ones like disappointment, pessimism, or impatience, are fear-based. When it comes right down to the nitty-gritty of it, God is **all natural**. Therefore, all negative emotion is **unnatural**. The natural part of you, your true nature, is your God-Self.

Remember our discussion of ego and how we allow it to "mask" the real God-Self. The fear-based emotions we hold within produce limitations and restrictions; because the ego holds on to them for dear life, literally. It doesn't want to lose control by letting them go. The ego was designed to cover our spiritual nature in this physical life. But if you so choose, you can release your negativity and, thereby, dissolve limitations and restrictions you have placed on yourself. The only prerequisite necessary is the desire to do so.

Making the **conscious choice** to release your negative emotions, feelings, and beliefs is the first and most important part of the process. When you make this choice and follow though with action, you will be enabling yourself. You will be more able to express and receive love. You will feel more love for yourself and for everyone around you. You will be consciously expressing from your God-Self, rather than your ego. Love being expressed from within to others, with no expectation of returns, is happiness.

The negative emotions, feelings, and false beliefs that you have been carrying are hidden in your subconscious mind and have been controlling your life. *It is time to let them go.* You will be creating a new way of life, a new way of thinking. You will move toward continuous, *conscious* creativity, without the burden of long-held negativity. If nothing more were to happen, you would be amazed how unencumbered you feel, how light, how free.

I can imagine that God is excited that you are willing to do this. So am I. Your rewards are limitless.

*   *   *

Emotional Release

There are several emotional release techniques, some of which can be *conducted on oneself.* Until a few years ago, I had never heard of any of them. Along with, perhaps, a good part of our American society, I assumed the only way to get rid of the emotions that cause us trouble was to go to a therapist of some kind. Please, do not infer from what I say that I am criticizing other therapies of any kind. I don't know enough about most of them to even have a "half-baked" opinion. I do know, however, that there are fewer success stories than we would like from those therapies that can cost quite a bit of money. The technique I use is *free*, and I perform it on myself.

I have used and examined several release techniques. I've discovered the most simple one works best for me. Some techniques are just too elaborate. This is not to say the technique I discuss is the best or the only one that works. I am simply saying that it is the one I use and find effective for me. I hope you will find it effective, too. If it does not give you what you want, I list other resources for information in Appendix V. There are many that are effective.

The power of the negative emotion is stored in our subconscious mind and retrieved when needed. When we release negative emotions with our negative reactions, we are actually rearranging the energy in our bodies. Negative emotions disrupt our energy systems. When we clear the emotion, our energy is more balanced. The power of the negative emotion is neutralized and disappears into a storage bin, so to speak, in our consciousness and is no longer the emotion that comes up when a similar situation recurs. When our mind and body have balanced energy, everything in our lives works better.

In the last chapter you made a list of your negative emotions, feelings, and beliefs. You also added bad and negative situations to the list. Pick any one of those feelings, emotions, or situations. It can be anger, anxiety, jealousy, unworthiness, rejection, resentment, or whatever you choose. It can relate to an upcoming interview, a job review, any kind of problem or anxiety. There is a false belief or limitation about yourself attached to every negative emotion or belief. For example, you can have a belief that you are unworthy of financial success. I suggest, when you begin, perhaps choose one that gives you only small problems. In this way you can build up your confidence and belief.

You can get results just by releasing the emotion, without first knowing what the belief is beneath it. You can also get two for one, and sometimes more, when you release the belief, without knowing the definite emotion in mind. The suggestion is this: work on releasing anything you feel is negative about yourself, whether it is an emotion, a feeling, or a belief.

Meridian Tapping Technique

Of the many types of emotional release techniques, I have been working with what is called a *meridian tapping technique*. There are several other meridian tapping techniques, but I have primarily used one called the Emotional Freedom Technique (EFT). This technique was originally developed by Gary Craig. Craig states, "The cause of all negative emotions is a disruption in the body's energy system." As we have stated earlier in our discussion, the entire body is energy. Thought is energy. Positive thought flows freely, and negative thought disrupts the free-flowing energy at all levels. The practice of chiropractic is a modality used to keep the body's main energy system functioning as a free-flowing device. No matter where we turn now, science is proving the theory that we are energy beings. Negative feelings can now be clinically shown to cause disruption in the brain. Our bodies use electrical energy in its function, as can be seen on medical diagnosis machines like EEG's and EKG's.

EFT was developed using information that is more than 5,000 years old. The energy system found by the ancient Chinese is a complex system of meridian points, located throughout the body, and is the foundation of a wide variety of health practices, including acupuncture and acupressure. EFT uses the meridian points of the body to release negative energy and realign the system to one of unobstructed free-flowing (positive) energy. By simply tapping near or on the end points of these energy meridians, you can experience some deep changes to your emotional and physical health. That's what EFT is all about. It has proven to be an effective emotional release therapy, used for over thirty years by hundreds of thousands of people. It is simple, easy to do, free, and can be done on oneself.

I have found that if one wants to be truly successful in creating a happier, more joyful life, this practice will be a life-long, daily endeavor. In my own experience, I have released emotional pain, slights, anger, and disappointments, one by one. Changing the emotions of fear to those of love increases our happiness and feelings of joy. This can be, for many of us, a new way of living our life. I will continue to work at releasing negativity until I am rid of every negative thought and emotion I can find; because the more I do it, the better and happier my life has become. None of us by ourselves can save the world; but by turning our fears to love, we can change our own little part of the world.

Originally, I was not going to include a discussion of emotional release in this book. However, I have found such success with it, in such a short time, that I felt it was imperative to share it with you. I am going to share only what is called The Basic Recipe, which is what I primarily use. I now feel that this should be an integral part in everyone's quest to make life better. I have made some small changes in the original technique used by Craig. If you want more information, and it is free, Appendix V has a reference you can use to go in-depth and learn everything from the founder, directly.

Below are the simple steps you can take to release some negative emotions from your subconscious. I will state here that there are sometimes some emotions buried too deeply to be released by this method. Those emotions could take some more intense work. Check the information on the EFT website, if that should be necessary in your case. But, be assured that you can do much to relieve some of the emotional reactions you have to specific issues in your life.

Releasing Statement of Intent

Before starting any release session, state, preferably out loud, "God, we will release this negative situation." This technique uses our connection to God (our God-Self) as an *essential* part of the process. Many emotional release techniques do not include this step. I believe it to be very important.

Set-up Statement

Next is the set-up statement. I prefer to write this statement down, so I can refer to it while tapping. *Please Note--Very Important:* The set-up statements may seem like negative statements to you, and they are. It is intended this way. It is one place where positive statements do not work. To quote the founder of EFT, "This is essential, because it is the negative that creates the energy disruptions (zzzzzts) that The Basic Recipe clears (and thus brings peace to the system). By contrast, conventional methods and popular self-help books stress positive thinking and preach avoiding the negative. This sounds good; but for our purposes it does little more than cover over the negative with pleasant-sounding words. EFT, on the other hand, needs to aim at the negative, so it can be neutralized. This allows our natural positives to bubble up to the top."

The set-up statement is one that declares the problem or negative emotion you wish to release. I illustrate some set-up statements below, shown as the underlined phrase. When writing this phrase we have two goals: 1) *acknowledge the problem* and 2) *accept and love yourself, in spite of it*. We do this by saying (again, out loud if possible, but not necessary):

- "Even though I have this _____, I deeply and completely accept myself."

The <u>underlined area</u> is the problem or emotion you want to release, so you can insert the words you need in that space. Some further examples of issues that might need change:

- Eating problem:
  "Even   though I have this <u>eating problem</u>, I deeply and completely accept myself."
- Difficulty making free throws:
  "Even though I have <u>difficulty making free throws</u>, I deeply and completely accept myself"
- Shoulder pain:
  "Even though I have this <u>shoulder pain</u>, I deeply and completely accept myself."
- Feelings of anger:
  "Even though I have these <u>feelings of anger</u>, I deeply and completely accept myself."
- Feelings of unworthiness:
  "Even though I have <u>feelings of unworthiness</u>, I deeply and completely accept myself."

Rating The Emotion

Let's take one of the above statements as a sample: "Even though I have this <u>eating problem</u>, I deeply and completely accept myself." Say the statement out loud and gauge your feelings about this problem. Take as long as necessary. On a scale of zero to 10, with 10 being the worst, where do you feel the emotion associated with the eating problem ranks? Visualize the problem at the same time as you say it. It might take a few minutes to get a good idea of how you would gauge it. Try to make it vivid in your mind. Then, to the best of your ability, give the emotion a number ranking.

Tapping Procedure

Now we begin the tapping procedure. Go to the tapping illustrations in Appendix III. We will start with the Karate Chop point, the first of nine points. Using whichever hand is more comfortable, lightly make a fist. You will use the four fingers of the other hand to tap the area of your fist between the base of the little finger and the wrist, on the outside edge of your hand, as your bent fingers face you. While tapping say, "Even though I have this eating problem, I deeply and completely accept myself."

While slowly saying the statement, tapping at the same time, put as much *loving emotion* as possible behind your statement. Tap seven or more times. In the same manner, you will then tap the other eight points shown on the illustrated figure.

There will be nine points in all: (1) Karate Chop point on side of hand, (2) top of head, (3) center end of either eyebrow, (4) outside corner of either eye, (5) bone edge directly under either eye, (6) point under tip of nose, (7) center under lower lip, above chin, (8) sternum, about ½" below Adam's Apple at u-point above breastbone, down 1" and right or left 1", (9) rib under armpit. . .point even with nipple in men and in approximately the middle of the bra for women, on the side of the body, again using the four fingers.

Re-gauge Emotion Rating

After each sequence, pause and become still for a moment. Repeat the set-up phrase, "Even though I have this eating problem, I deeply and completely accept myself." See how your feelings have changed. Think about your former eating problem for a few moments and rate the feeling with the same ranking scale of zero to 10. Reaching 0 is the goal, and you may have to do more than one sequence to release all of the negative feelings and emotions related to the initial problem. Most people get a lower reading after the first sequence. You may do these tapping routines as many times as you wish, as well as releasing as many emotions in a row as you wish.

If you do not get the results you want on the first sequence of tapping, repeat the entire sequence as many times as it takes to get relief. Some emotions may be stubborn, and some may release easily. If an issue becomes stubborn, you may have to investigate other methods of finding your deeply-held emotions. This, too, is discussed on Craig's EFT web site. I have put links and web addresses in Appendix V for you to refer to, if you wish.

Persistence is a big key here. If you feel uncomfortable in *any* way, it may be a sign of your inner resistance to letting this emotion go. If you truly want it gone, keep at it!

Thank God for the Release

I suggest one last important step. When you finish each emotion or problem release, I suggest you say something similar to the following: "Thank you, God, for releasing my problem with _____." Fill in the blank with the problem, person, situation, health issue, or feeling you have released. Further, I recommend that you use this as a gratitude statement for a few days after the release. This reminds your energy system that it is gone and no longer of consequence.

Reinforcement Tapping

When you have reduced the emotion rating down to the 0 - 2 range, reinforcing with positive affirmation statements will do a great deal to reduce them further and at the same time keep the negative emotions from creeping back into mind. You may use this method any time you get urgings for any negative action.

Example: When you start to think about eating, and you know you have no real physical hunger. In these sessions you do not need to use the setup statement.

Do the entire tapping routine as described above starting with the KC point. When tapping use positive statements reinforcing what ever it is you are working on. Such as:

- I choose to eat correctly
- I choose to be aware of everything I eat
- I enjoy eating less and feeling better
- Thank you for removing the pain
- It's easy and fun to eat less
- I am feeling more joy in my life
- I love myself and express this love to others

There are others releasing sources you may research and are listed in Appendix V.

Chapter 18
Meditation

To the mind that is still, the whole universe opens to them." This was said over 3000 years ago by Lao Tzu. Today, I say the phrase, "Be still and know I am God." To me, these two statements say the same thing. In Tzu's statement, the universe is God.

We are here to discuss a tool that, if used, can help make your life better. And that's why we're here, isn't it? It's about creating a more satisfying life for yourself, either in a small way or a large way. Meditation can be used to whatever degree you choose. You can take just a few minutes out of your day to release some stress. Or, you can get more serious about it, by devoting more work and time to it. Your choice.

I think of meditation as being either *passive* or *active*, and it can be approached either way, or in combination. There are many wonderful books available on the subject of meditation. I have read many, but not all. The books I have read primarily discuss what I would call a more passive approach to meditation, one of relaxation, quieting the mind, and (perhaps) listening. This method, when defined as passive, would not be entered into for the purpose of necessarily receiving information, which I will further discuss as an active meditation.

When thinking in terms of either passive or active, I believe meditation needs to be entered into with a conscious intention. Are you going to meditate to simply quiet your mind and relieve some stress? Or, are you going to meditate more actively, by thinking about something and listening for answers? These are two different approaches.

Passive Meditation

If your goal is simply to become more relaxed and calm, meditation can be used for that purpose. It is probably the most simple way to instantly find a little peace. As a stress reliever, meditation has been found to be most effective. There have been numerous scientific studies that have *proven* that the brain physically changes during and after meditation; and if the brain changes, so does the rest of the body. However, that kind of brain change would usually involve sessions of about 20 minutes or more. But even a five- to ten-minute session would be worth the effort. You will be glad you did. This is another one of those times, however, when once will not tell the tale. Again, that word *persistence*. There will always be those who say they don't have time. How valuable is a few minute's peace to you? You are so very much worth a few minutes, if that is all you have.

You don't have to sit in a lotus position. You don't have to hold your thumbs to your middle fingers, with your palms facing upward. You don't have to be in a room by yourself. In its most basic form, meditation can simply entail sitting still, in a relaxed position, closing your eyes, and turning off your thoughts. Don't fret about your thoughts. The simplest thing to do in that regard is to just repeat a word, such as "peace," slowly and with feeling. Just focusing on the word "peace" will help you feel it. You can focus on your breathing, or not. The point is to not be distracted. You could do this at your desk, when it's only for a few minutes. A couple of times a day could work wonders for you. Perhaps, more than a coffee break could.

If you're able to spend more than five to ten minutes, do what you can to improve your outside environment. Find a quiet place. Perhaps, play some soft background music, if that is to your liking and not distracting. (I have a TV cable music channel that plays nothing but this type of music 24/7. It's wonderful and has facilitated my experiencing many profound moments when I wasn't expecting them.)

If you are willing and able to spend more than a few minutes in meditation and might be looking for a more spiritual experience, one that goes beyond relaxation and stress relief, I recommend stating to yourself and the universe what your intention is. Perhaps you have been experiencing an ongoing, stressful situation in your life, and you're just plain needing some comfort and assurance that all is well. Go into your meditation with the *conscious intention* of finding that comfort and assurance. God knows how you are feeling. The God-Self in you is always waiting for you to turn within. That is, in my belief, what meditation is really all about--turning within--going to that place in you that always, *always* knows peace. That peace is waiting to come out and manifest itself in your life. If you go searching, with the belief that it is there, it can't help but appear.

Meditation is but one of many ways to reach that part of you that I have called your God-Self. When you become able to touch that essence, and become aware of being *one* with that essence, your life can change, in small ways and in large ways. I have personally always thought of it as "touching Spirit."

I am trying to promote the idea of a passive form of meditation that can be as simple as I have described above. I want this notion of meditation to be as simple as possible for you, if you are not already involved with it. I'm not really here to discuss all the various types. I simply want you to know that meditation can be so easy and so productive in making your life more peaceful, and that can't help but be a better life. Can it? Quite frankly, I haven't tried all the various forms of meditation. My goal here is, as I have said before, KIS (keep it simple).

If you are interested in more of the many types of meditation, there are so many books and web sites available. Please see Appendix V for a list of some of them.

Active Meditation or Talking with God

Active meditation involves conscious thought and conscious intention, seeking results and answers to life's questions. Simply defined, active meditation is a way to contact Universal Consciousness for information and inspiration. In its final analysis, it is a conversation with God. I use this meditation method as a tool of creativity, when I need answers to specific questions. It is my way of accessing my God-Self, my inner power and intelligence (all are God). The more I contact God, the closer I am to *being* God.

When I say I use active meditation as a creative tool, I do not mean just in the context of creating something tangible. I believe this type of meditation to be very helpful in creating a "new me." Sometimes there is something that just needs to be changed, an idea, an attitude, an emotional reaction, etc. My conversation with God is truly about getting the best advice and information there is to be had. It is going directly to the Source.

Reducing distractions and becoming more focused in a deeper mind state allows answers (inspiration) to come to me more easily and with more clarity. There are many meditation techniques covered in books and on the internet. This is, however, a different type of meditation. My meditative method is the one I wish to share, because it has worked so well for me. Also, it is easy and simple to do. It allows me to share what I believe to be my soul's purpose as a messenger.

If you agree to, or are willing to at least consider, the premise that you are God and that all His power, wisdom, and love are within you, then this means you are simply accessing the knowledge you already own and have available. To me, it is a matter of belief. If you believe, to some degree, that you are God and are one with Him, then you become Him. This belief changes the parameters of everything. It changes the way you perceive the world, as well as how you act and think. When you change your perception and your thinking, you change your life.

I believe God designed us with the skills to reach Him easily, without a lifetime of contemplative study. He is very intelligent. He did not give us these tools just for grins and giggles. There was purpose and unlimited intelligence behind the design. Ancient spiritual wisdom says the same thing. "The knowledge we need is within us." Everything we need for human happiness and a successful human life is within. In order to create the life we desire, we need only use the tools that are right in front of us. I believe that God designed the system to reflect the KIS method. It is we humans who have complicated the process. We need to learn to get out of our own way.

For many years throughout my lifetime I meditated in an erratic pattern, off and on. I was operating under the false belief that the only way I could be successful in communicating with God the way I wanted, would take many years and was best done in a high-mountain monastery. Guess what? Ain't so! I now meditate quite easily, and I believe that is because I found the way that was meant to benefit me the most. I guess the God in me knew that.

When I accepted that there might be another way and released the false belief that it was difficult, it all came together rather easily. As we move through life experience, there are moments when a dawning, or a light bulb of realization, indicates truths to us. We become aware, at a more conscious level, of what works for us.

The realization that I could really carry on a conversation with God (my God-Self) happened for me while I was in a session of meditative emotional release. I was lying quietly, as had been instructed, and I asked God to help me release the negative emotion of anger into my hand, which I was holding over my heart. I did not get the releasing reaction I had been told to expect. I then said to myself, "Why don't I get the results others get?" Obviously, this was a negative statement, but a positive thought came back to me anyway. "But you did." My next thought was, "How do you figure that? I didn't feel what they said I would feel." The answering thought was, "How does the anger feel now?" So I asked myself, "Do I feel less anger now?" Sure enough, the answer I received was, "Yes!" The "yes" did not come to me audibly, but most definitely in the form of thought. And I was, at that time, very much in the listening mode of active meditation. I think that is very important here. By *intentionally asking*, and then *intentionally listening*, the answers come.

After that experience with receiving answers, I looked at meditation in a completely different way. I became consciously aware that meditation did not mean I always had to dispense with all thought and find the silence between the thoughts, in order to contact God. I discovered that being in a meditative state could help me be a "better listener," more receptive to God's inspiration. I believe this is due to the fact that in the meditative state our brain waves slow down, which allows much higher clarity.

It was also at this time that I had another light bulb moment. I was more acutely aware that what I was hearing was coming from inside me. I saw how I could talk to my Higher Self anytime I wanted, just by being still, relaxing, *asking*, and *listening*.

This is the way it works for me, and I have discovered it works for others in a similar fashion. There are many ways to communicate with the God Force within. You may have to try various question and answer methods until you find the one that works best for you. If you do not already have a method, start with the one I use and then make changes if you need to. Most importantly, trust yourself in this process. Remember who you are, visualize the God within you, and She will become true for you.

During active meditation you are going to talk to God. Talk to Him as a friend, mentor, or teacher. Trust in God and in yourself. You will find that He will give you all the information and inspiration you seek, freely and with love.

Most certainly, talking with God can cause you no harm. God only gives positive, helpful, loving information. If the message received is negative in nature, it is coming from your ego. Negative information is tied to negative emotions and beliefs. If this should happen, you lovingly release the negative thoughts and emotions and start again.

Talking to God is a way to realize who and what we really are. We are all God, and God is Love. We were not meant to struggle and sacrifice. We were not meant to live lives of fear. However, we falsely believe that this is how it is supposed to be. When we take action to practice being who we really are, we will begin to live who we really are; and then the creation of all our desires will come automatically. When we become more of our God-Self, we attract and experience only the good, leaving the negative behind. This may seem like a "far out" concept, but human experience shows that this works. Everything different or new has a starting point. This is that point.

My Meditation Exercise for Relaxation

I use both passive and active meditations with each session. You can, of course, do any combination that you would like, depending on what you are trying to accomplish. To begin my relaxation, I use a method that was first designed by Herbert Benson, a Harvard University MD. It is called the Relaxation Response and has been taught since the early 70's to professionals all over the world, who have then taught it to their patients.

When the Relaxation Response or other similar methods are practiced for as little as 15 minutes, twice a day, not only will brain chemistry change for the better, but there can be permanent changes to the body, as well.

I meditate every morning before getting up and every evening before going to bed. (The frequency of your practice is entirely up to you.) In the early morning I find that I am already nearly totally relaxed. I stay in bed, because I do not have any trouble staying awake. If you are afraid you will fall back to sleep, then by all means get up and move to a comfortable chair. Choose a quiet space without distractions, with low or no light.

Before starting, select a positive word, phrase, or sound that you will repeat as you meditate. I call this the focus word or phrase. Use words like "peace," "one," "God," or "love," or sounds, such as "om," or hum. By choosing affirmations like "I am peace," "I am love," or "I am perfect health," you can get the benefit of saying an affirmation at the same time. Choosing whatever is comfortable for you is best. The primary function of the words or sound is to focus your mind on only one thought, making it easier to dismiss other thoughts. You will use this word or phrase after you have accomplished relaxation.

After finding a comfortable position, close your eyes. First, take three slow, deep breaths. At this point, you will be focusing your attention on your body. Starting with your toes, gently ask them to relax. You will then ask the foot to relax, then the calf, and so forth, up to the head and neck. Visualize each body part as you focus your attention on that body part. See it, perhaps, melting into your bed or chair. As you practice, you will quickly see that it takes a shorter period of time to accomplish relaxation.

When you are relaxed, begin to slowly repeat the positive word or sound you had previously chosen. Do this with as much positive emotion and feeling as you can attach to the word. Keep repeating the word in your mind.

When repeating words or affirmations, here is another trick I learned from a hypnotist. When saying the words, roll your closed eyes up in your head and hold them there for as long as possible. At first this can be a strain, but it gets easier with practice. Brain studies show that while doing this eye roll, the brain almost immediately drops down to the alpha brain wave level and will hold there as long as you are relaxed. In scientific research studies the alpha brain wave level is considered to be the meditative level. It is the creative, imaginative state. At this level of brain wave activity, less sensory data enters the nervous system from the environment.

If random thoughts pop into your mind, lovingly let them go by, and just say to yourself, "oh well" or "whoops," and go back to repeating the word or phrase. When thoughts appear, do not judge them or yourself. Don't be concerned about them. These thoughts are normal, and there is no way to completely avoid them. However, with use of your focus words you will find that fewer of them appear as your sessions progress. While repeating the phrase, I have personally found that visualizing a simple scene, or the word itself, will dramatically reduce random thoughts. I use flowers, beaches, and mountains. After a while, the scene or word visual becomes rote; and the body will relax and focus even better.

Keep repeating the word or phrase for ten to fifteen

minutes, or longer if you wish. At this point you have fulfilled the passive portion of the exercise. You may continue on into the active meditation, or you may stop here, continue your day, or slip off to sleep. If you are stopping here, then stop the word or sound repetition and spend a few moments being still. Then, open your eyes and continue relaxing, while identifying and enjoying the feeling of less stress. Thank God for all those things you have that are good in your life. You are now done.

Active Meditation Exercise

You can practice this active exercise either by itself or as a continuation of the meditation exercise I described above.

It would be a good idea, if you have a question to present to your God-Self, to write that question down and keep it near your place of meditation. If you have it close, you can later write down answers, if you wish.

If you do not choose to engage in the more extensive relaxation described above, at least spend a few minutes getting relaxed, using whatever form of relaxation technique you choose. Begin this part of the exercise by repeating to yourself slowly three times, "Be still and know I am God."

At this point I visualize a star or burst of light within me, full of vibrating energy. I locate this star just below my breast bone, in the center of my chest. This visualization, while not necessary, can be very helpful, as it dramatically improves your feeling of oneness with the power within. Holding the picture of this energy, I then repeat an "I am God" affirmation. (Change if you wish.) This is mine:

"I am God.

I was created by God, out of God, to be God in perfect human form.

I am all that God is.

God is everything, everywhere.

God is energy.

God's energy is in every cell of my body.

God's energy is power, wisdom, and love.

I am God."

Now, feeling centered, take a moment to bring forward the question you want to discuss. Still with eyes closed and relaxed, ask the question. Example: "God, I need ideas on how I can become the head buyer in my purchasing department. I am qualified and competent. What ideas do you have for the accomplishment of my desire?" Be still and allow answers to come. One of two things will happen at this point. You will immediately have a thought. When you address a new issue or question, the first thought is the most important and most relevant to you. Listen as well as you can at this point, and focus on what you receive in the way of an answer. Of course, the thought will be either positive or negative.

First, we will handle a negative thought. If your first thought is negative, spend absolutely no time judging it. This negative thought is almost always related to a negative feeling or false belief, which has not been released. It needs to be released before moving on.

These are some thoughts that might come up:

- "You're not qualified enough." (Even though you are very well-qualified.)
- "You do not have enough training."
- "They will probably choose someone else over me."
- "I'm the wrong race."
- "I'm too heavy."
- "I'm not good-looking enough."

Subconsciously, you may not believe you are worthy of the position, or you might have the false belief that you do not deserve it. Or, there could be some other negative emotion or belief blocking you. Harboring negative emotions and beliefs deep in the subconscious mind is the most common reason for people not getting what they desire. Every human alive carries some kind of negative emotional baggage. If the truth be known, each of us probably carries a ton of it. It is my strong belief that if you do not release the negativity that is presently managing your thought and action, replacing it with love, it is like beating your head against the wall. You just won't get to where you want to go.

I recommend releasing the negative emotions immediately, whenever you encounter them. You have found a negative belief or emotion that is blocking this particular desire. Go back to Chapter 17 and work on releasing the emotion that is causing this negative feeling. Having released your negative block/s, when you return to your meditation and your question to your God-Self, you will find it much easier to hear positive answers.

Now, after again spending a couple of minutes getting relaxed, return to the meditation and resume your conversation with God. Ask the question again, "God, I need ideas on how I can become the head buyer in my purchasing department. I am qualified and competent. What ideas do you have for the accomplishment of my desire?" Listen for the first thought. If the first answer is positive, give it your focused attention. Focusing your attention allows you to open to Universal Consciousness, and the ideas will begin to flow.

The act of talking to God is deliberate creation. Talk to God as a trusted friend or mentor. You must have the willingness to believe and act upon that which is given you. I have never had an incidence where the information I received and acted upon ever caused me harm of any kind. I act upon only what I consider to be loving thoughts. Negative thoughts are easy to identify. They are the ones that can cause problems, because they are coming from the ego portion of personality.

Write down answers that come to you, so that you can refer to them later. You may certainly stop to write, and then return to your meditation. Take the ideas given to you on the specific question and act upon them. If you feel an answer refers to some other issue you have, write that down, also, and follow through with action. That's just an added bonus.

The solution may be as simple as how you have been acting toward others at work. In fact, just releasing the negative emotions is likely to change your attitude at work; and you may quickly see changes in the situation and the people around you.

This will be, yet again, an exercise in persistence. Don't give up, if you don't feel it worked as well as you would have liked at first. Keep at it. There are answers within you. They belong to you. Please, believe that! God has answers and wants nothing more than for you to hear them, trust them, and act upon them.

Further Uses for Active Meditation

The uses for the meditation tool are endless, literally. The questions and conversations can be on any subject. Do not be shy. God does not judge. You can ask for and receive information on how to create better health, release negative emotions, improve relationships, or find solutions to business or work challenges. You could receive direction on how to proceed with some artistic endeavor. Active meditation is a form of prayer, a different type than is thought of as prayer by most people. You are not asking God to intervene and solve a problem for you (a prayer of supplication). You are asking for inspiration and information, so that you can take responsibility and create your life as you choose.

I suggest you work on one opportunity or challenge, and its solution, at a time. Once you receive the information and form a plan and act upon it, you can look for more information on different subjects. No positive request is too big or too small. God wants to help; that is what She does.

Let's say you have an idea that you want a relationship of some kind, a new job, or anything else new in your life. During active meditation you simply state to God, "I would like to have _____." God is an unlimited source of ideas. From the time you start a desired creation, all thoughts about the creation are a string of ideas that you use to create a plan and act upon that plan. If you run into a problem or roadblock during creation, go back to the source and say, "God, I have a problem here. What do I do next?" or "How can I remove this roadblock?" *Expect* to receive answers. They are there. And, be sure to use your tool of gratitude.

A really positive and powerful way to use active meditation is to find and then release stored negative emotion. Emotional release was discussed in the last chapter. This is yet another technique for release.

During an active mediation simply ask, "God, what are the negative emotions that I need to release?" I have found when asking this question, I can get bombarded with answers. As I said before, we have a great deal of negative false beliefs, feelings, and emotions. If you ask God what they are, and then release them, this, by itself, can unleash great positive forces in your life. Inspiration can start coming at you that you have not asked for yet. Good will come into your life automatically when you express good to the world around you. It is as simple as that.

Use active meditation to unleash your imagination. For example, when I build a website, either for myself or a client, I build it in my head first, while in meditation. I ask God for help by saying, "Hey, God, help me with this project, OK?" His ideas flood my mind; and I use them to visualize the form of the site, the headlines, the copy, the art work. I picture everything about the project as completed and finished. With God's ideas I get it just the way I want it in my head. You will find God is very skillful at helping you *intentionally* co-create. When you create in this manner, you are getting thoughts and ideas directly from Universal Consciousness. It is your choice whether to use them or not, but I believe you will be pleased with the results.

Active meditation is very effective in planning any upcoming event; i.e., a job interview. In the deep meditative state use visualization to picture exactly how you want the interview or other event to go. This is particularly effective in sales situations. Universal Consciousness will show you a perfect scenario and exactly what should happen to make it a success. When combined with other tools like emotional release and visualization, people can become super salespeople; because they lose all of their fear. Anything you wish to create will be easier to manifest with meditation. People who meditate over time have been found to have a higher awareness of self and their relationship to their environment.

I used meditation a great deal as a tool to accomplish this book. Every time I got stuck or confused about how I wanted to proceed, I meditated my way through it. God gave me this book, but I think that most books are created with His help, consciously or unconsciously.

Gratitude is powerful. I suggest an entire meditation once a week on just gratitude. I thank God for anything that might come to mind; such as, "Thank you for my perfect health," "Thank you for the financial abundance you gave me today," "Thank you for the idea about visualization."

With practice you will find meditation becomes second nature, and you will miss it if you do not do it every day. As implausible as all this might sound, it works.

Communicating with God, like any skill, takes practice and persistence; but if you want it to work, it will. Becoming good at this is no different than acquiring any other skill. Using this skill is rather like a snowball rolling downhill, accumulating snow as it goes. The more you work at it, the greater your trust. The greater your trust, the more you believe. The more you believe, the better it works. The better it works, the greater your success. The greater your success, the more firm your belief. Around we go again, and it just keeps increasing.

Sometimes the conversations can get intense, and you might begin to believe God is a big blabbermouth. God cannot wait to communicate with you, however, and is available 24/7. It's God's nature to be inspiring (in-Spirit). It is who He is. As humans, we don't always listen well. This meditation form helps us to purposely focus on that "listening," putting us in a better position of receiving.

As a tool of creation, meditation, used its many ways, is the most effective I have ever found

CHAPTER 19
Visualization

Since humanoids were endowed with souls, Universal Consciousness has been sending out ideas as thoughts; and we have made choices as what to do with those ideas. An idea is omnipresent throughout Consciousness, but only a few receive it and do something with it. Each of us has received untold numbers of ideas and thoughts we have chosen not to entertain any further. If we attach more thought to new ideas, and then follow through with even more thought and some action, we create all we experience, computers, airplanes, books, Disney Parks, our education system, our relationships, our vocations. All things and all experiences began with an idea in someone's imagination.

Visualization is one of the tools we use in the natural progression of creation. We may very well be using it without thinking too much about it, unconsciously, but we do hold pictures in our minds all the time. If you are going to build a birdhouse, you would probably have a *picture of your idea* of a birdhouse in your mind, before you start. In the process of creating a trip to the zoo, you would probably picture the zoo, or the route you would drive to the zoo, rather than just holding the *idea of the zoo* in your mind. Just try thinking of a zoo, without having a picture of it! If you are wanting a date with a specific person, you would quite naturally hold some picture in your mind of being with that person. Again, try to think of that person without the mind picture. You are getting the idea by now, I'm sure. The screen of your mind is always working, even in your dreams.

An old saying says a picture is worth a thousand words. Perhaps, a *crystal-clear visualization* is worth 100,000 words, or even more. An idea visualized, whether big or small, will be taken by the universe and forged into the manifestation of that idea. For practice, just imagine taking an idea from God and, with additional thought and desire, turn it into a new mode of transportation, using only compressed air as a fuel source. This new idea will transport man in light-weight vehicles around the earth at very high speeds without any pollution. Someday, someone will take an idea like this and do more than make a cartoon out of it. In the realm of unlimited possibilities, if you can *see* it, really picture it, it can become a physical reality.

Visualization is a mental, visual plan played in the mind. Jack Nicklaus, a Hall of Fame golfer, used this technique to win eighteen major championships, 73 PGA Tour wins, and 10 Champions Tour wins. He played every round in his head, before taking the course. Once on the course, he visualized every shot, before every swing. His mind was so well-trained, it took him no time at all to do this as he played a round.

Let's work on creating something here, something you *really* want. It can be an invention, a relationship, a new car, a vacation trip, or whatever your mind conjures up. Soar with your imagination!

Optimally, you have a few minutes to do this. Again, optimally, close your eyes and focus on being relaxed. Even better, use visualization while in active meditation. Take whatever time you need to *feel good*. Begin to form in your mind a picture of your dream. We're looking for as much clarity here as you can muster.

(You will get better with practice.) Visualize as many details of your idea as you can, the more the better. Include in your picture what things will look like for you (and others, if others are involved) when your dream comes about, as well as how you will feel. These feelings will add *immense* power to your creation. Every time you think about this dream, remember these feelings. And, if you are able, don't forget sound and other sensory input. (Obviously, that goes beyond *visual*-ization, but it adds to the imagined experience, if you are able to do it.)

Create the picture in your mind like a movie and, perhaps, even draw a picture of it on paper. A drawing of stick figures and funny looking objects would even help. If there are pictures available in a magazine or on the internet that remind you of what you want to accomplish, use those, too. These could include faces that express joy. (Because you will feel joy and happiness when this happens, right?) You need not be an accomplished artist; God does not require a Monet-quality painting. He understands stick figures just fine. Carry your picture in your pocket or handbag and look at it often. When you look at your picture and think your thoughts about this manifestation that is taking place, and this is important, state either out loud or silently, "Thank you, God, for bringing this to me now."

Feel the gratitude. Use the power, wisdom, and love of God to help you realize that it is *already* in your possession, in some dimension you perhaps cannot see; but it is there. This is called *faith*. The more you think about the idea you wish to create, the better. Remember, thought is prayer, communication with God. If you think in terms of prayer, practice the prayer of thanksgiving more than the prayer of supplication. It is far more effective. It is an affirmation prayer, expressing your belief that what you want is coming to you.

118

You can train your mind to visualize anything, just by practicing. (Again, persistence!) There have been countless stories passed around about athletes who use visualization in their training routines, to great effect. As with the story of Jack Nicklaus' success with visualization, the subconscious mind doesn't know the difference between the actual physical motions of swinging the golf club and the mere mental picture of doing so.

Visualization is one of those skills you can practice anywhere, and no one will ever know. It is all in your head, on your own personal movie screen, and very private. Many people call this daydreaming; but whatever one calls it, visualization is a powerful creative tool. Visualization is a motion picture of thought.

You already visualize as a part of your thought process. We just normally form pictures in our mind of what we are thinking, at an unconscious level. But we are talking here about creating what you *want* in life, particularly in relation to a change, so a greater focus on *creative* visualization is the goal. Creative visualization is a *conscious, intentional* action of the mind.

Research studies have shown that visualized images play a more prominent role in *recall* than just the written word. In other words, if you were to see a scene in a movie, you would remember it more accurately than if you had read the same scene in a book. The visual image further impacts the experience in the brain. (Auditory messages enhance the experience even more, especially for some people.)

Visualization can be used in conjunction with other mind techniques, such as relaxation, meditation, or affirmations. When you are attempting to relax, a mind picture of a waterfall, the breaking surf, or your body parts turning to jelly, can't help but facilitate relaxation. Let your imagination go. Use visualization, consciously and intentionally, whenever you can. Believe it will work, because it can. Don't let others dissuade you of its effectiveness.

Remember this: Visualizing what you *don't want* is as effective as visualizing what you *do want*. Unfortunately, most of us, far too often, do just that. We rehearse what we don't want, over and over and over. It is your choice what you want to see happen.

The human was designed to experience through our senses of touch, sight, sound, smell, and taste. We can use these senses in our imagination, as well as physically. Our ability to do this is a gift. Using them in our mind, as with visualization, helps our creation process. We experience in our mind, as well as physically, and we can direct how we are going to do that. That is the power given us. As God, the Creative Force, we are innately able to create what we want.

Starting with the first idea and thought of what you desire, use your conscious visualization, in combination with all the tools you have been given. Thought is prayer. Visualized thought is prayer on steroids. Sit back, relax, and create your script in mind movies, with stereo sound, and all the special effects you can imagine. *SEE* it as you want it. Life is fun! Enjoy!

Chapter 20
Gratitude

When trying to create something in your life that you do not presently see, whether it is a change in a personal habit or way of thinking, or a new home, the expression of gratitude may seem to be something that comes *after* the new creation appears. We, perhaps, see only the polite sequence of "please". . .action. . ."thank you."

Good manners are really swell, and I heartily believe in using them appropriately and sincerely. They make the world a better place. We all like to hear a "thank you" for some action we've taken or gift we've given to another.

But, I am not here to discuss good manners. I am taking the understanding of what gratitude is to a whole new realm, so to speak. . .the realm of your creative ability. Gratitude is far more than a mental thought process. I want you to think of gratitude as an aspect of *who you are*, a part of your very being. It is a part of your being that can help bring about true abundance in your life, abundance of every kind, not just money.

There are unlimited possibilities out there in the universe, just waiting for your belief and faith. We discussed in Chapter 15 how to create positive experience for yourself. We talked about how an idea of what you want is developed in a thought process, how to form a picture in your mind of your desire, and how to imagine the emotions you will feel when your creation is in place. We talked about doing what you can to express the belief that what you want is *already* here. Gratitude is the final step of this creation process. It is the step *beyond believing* in your creation and brings it about even more quickly.

Your desire may not be visible now, but it *is* in the quantum field of possibility, simply because you thought it. (The quantum field is another discussion entirely, but be assured that what you want *is* a "done deal.") Your job is simply to visualize it in your mind, believe it to be, and express gratitude for it. That expression of gratitude is a statement *affirming your expectation, receiving, and acceptance* of your desire, *knowing* it is coming to you. Yes, it is an act of faith, when you can't see the manifestation yet. But *feel* the gratitude anyway. Wear it like an outfit of clothing. Know that it flows through you, as does your blood.

We've talked here about how your gratitude will facilitate your creation process. But there is so much more your feelings and expressions of gratitude can do, just in your day-to-day journey. Your gratitude involves more than being thankful just for your own blessings. You also have the ability to express your gratitude so that it, in turn, will be a blessing to others.

Expressing gratitude to people for even the smallest acts is telling them that you appreciate them and what they do. And you can bet, to some degree, you are making their day better. Gratitude tells people you are paying attention to them, that you are present in that moment. Obviously, adding a smile to your "thank you" adds even more blessing to the statement. Consider trying to avoid the word "thanks," at least occasionally. Not that the word isn't valid, or that it's rude, or that it should never be used. Just think about how much more meaningful it sounds to hear a sincere, thoughtful "thank you," rather than the quick "thanks," which sometimes sounds so impersonal as to be a period at the end of a sentence. (Of course, it is always better than nothing.) It's the sincerity that counts. The sincerity takes mindfulness, being in the moment.

Scientific studies have shown that the brains of both the giver and the receiver of expressed gratitude are affected in a positive way. Brain wave activity changes. Body chemistry changes. And when those changes occur in our bodies, our health can improve. "Thank you" is a small statement, but with huge results, in the long term! Actually, that "scientific studies" business just reinforces two notions: 1) the mind and body are ever- connected, and 2) the habit of thinking positive thoughts improves health.

When you work towards a state of being more grateful, you will naturally realize how good it makes you feel. Feeling and expressing gratitude always puts you in a positive frame of mind, which is where you want to be all the time. Looking out there at the world around you, and finding more and more things to be grateful for, is a wonderful way to develop positive thinking habits.

Focusing on all the things you now enjoy and love in your life, and expressing to God your gratitude, is a very positive way to affirm your love for the world around you, as it is right now. Refer back to the list of all the good in your life, which you hopefully made while back in Chapter 16. Take five things off that list and thank God for each of them at least three times per day for a week. Observe how you feel after one week. Chances are very good that you will notice the difference in your positive outlook.

Thanking God for your good every day, as many times as possible, is getting the Law of Attraction into the act, as well. Remember, "like attracts like." Gratitude is the most powerful of attractors. More of the things you are grateful for will appear in your life, and you will constantly receive bonuses of happiness and other good stuff. It is impossible to feel and express gratitude too much. (If you express it out loud, perhaps others around you might learn from your example. That can only be good.) *What you think is who you are*, every minute of every day.

Express gratitude for even the smallest of things. . .your comfortable bed, your hot water tank, coffee or tea, stop signs and lights that keep you safe, the windshield wipers, pens that work, and so on. You can work yourself into a pretty wonderful state of mind just by getting your day started off this way. Imagine how good the rest of it will be.

Nourish your mind, your body, and your spirit with gratitude. It is addictive, but it's calorie-free and a natural energy food.

Chapter 21
Holding Your Creation In Mind

Your desired creation may be a more svelte you. It may be a new job. The process for facilitating your creation is the same, no matter the size of the dream. Your "life" is *everything* about you, your size, your relationships, a needed parking spot, *everything*. Creating *any* change involves the same process.

While your desired creation may not be quite on the scope of creating the universe, bringing it into your life will be accomplished by the same process used billions of years ago when God (we) created the universe. First came the idea. As that idea was held in mind, it became desire, and God formed a clear picture of His desire. He then spoke the word of His creation and affirmed it to be so. It then came forth into physical form. That same process is your part of creating what you want.

Inherent in the process of creation is holding the desire in mind. In your case, no matter the size of the creation, you must believe it to be possible and hold it in your mind.

Previously, I discussed how you are an actor in the play of life, and to date your life has unfolded exactly the way you've written it. If you do not like the script you have written (you weigh more than you like, you aren't pleased with your present job, you want to be more patient), sit down and rewrite it. If you like the script you have written, just add more love, peace, and harmony, and continue on. Hold your vision of the life you want to create in your mind. Think about it, visualize it, and talk about it the way you *want* it to be (not the way you do *not want* it to be).

Take the necessary human action to begin the creation. If, for example, you want to open a flower shop, think flowers. Think about everything you might need to open this retail store. Think about it with loving, positive thoughts only. Visualize people streaming into your store on Valentine's Day and Mother's Day. Visualize the layout, the flower coolers, the parking lot, and every other detail that comes to you. When new information or ideas appear, and they most certainly will, update your movie script.

Regardless of where you are in your life, you must take some kind of action to make it happen. If you are young, you might need training or education. A job in a flower shop would be good, too. If you have to take a job as a server in a restaurant, take it, and do it well. Always remember that even though it might not be your "career choice," it is keeping you on your path. Be grateful! Tell everyone you are going to open a flower shop. Let any job gift you with the opportunity for learning how to work with people. Learn all you can. Let all your experience be a gift. If you want this flower shop badly enough, and you don't have immediate funding for it, save all the money you can. Even a small nest egg will prove your desire is there. Keep looking for that job in a flower shop or the flower department of a large store, always keeping in mind your vision of what you desire.

Use all the tools we have discussed, affirmations, visualization, meditation. Think nothing but flower shop! Dream it, breathe it, and have it for breakfast. Ask anyone you can think of who might be able to help you. Talk to flower shop owners. Most people love to talk about their love and vision, too. Talk to bankers, look for a government grant, search the internet, and keep on thinking flowers. Hold in mind the love you feel for your dream. Believe in yourself and know that your hard work is worth it. You are worth it. You have every right to live your dream.

If roadblocks come up, find a way around them. Keep moving forward. Believe that what you need is there, and be alert for opportunities. Pay attention to everything around you. Ideas could come from anywhere. Follow up every lead you might receive in thought or from other people. Sometimes the most mundane of ideas are the ones that will lead directly to your desire. Investigate them all, even those that seem cloaked or covered. Depending on your age and present position in life, this could take a while, or it could happen very quickly. Feel your enthusiasm, but be relaxed in the idea that it will come.

Holding the thought of your idea and vision in mind will make it manifest. Keep using all the tools of the creation process. Don't let negativity and doubt creep in. Live with the mindset that you won't be defeated by anything.

Enjoy your life and be happy where you are now. The flower shop will not create happiness. Love creates happiness, and the flower shop provides you with something you love to do, while experiencing being human. No matter how many flower shops you might eventually own, your happiness can only come from within. Money and success do not create happiness. Love creates happiness within you. When your soul (love) is bubbling over, and love is everywhere in your life, happiness is there, no matter the circumstances.

Starting a new business is a big enterprise. Your dream may be to change something about yourself, something you have been unhappy with. Perhaps you have repeatedly tried to lose a few pounds.

The same process will apply in the creation of a thinner you. You've already had the idea that you want to lose weight, and you know the desire has come from that idea. You might have spoken your word, but here you must take responsibility for what your word has been. Have you been affirming yourself to be overweight? Have you complained how hard it is to lose weight? Do you hold a picture in your mind of you as you are now, believing it to be you forever? If your answer to these questions is "yes," then you need to go back to the desire part of the process and go on a new path.

That new path is this: Hold in mind what you *want*, what you really *want*. Up to now you might only have held in mind what you *don't want*. That will only hold that experience to you, like a magnet.

Use the tools of creating a new you that we have discussed. While you practice these tools, and I can't stress enough how important this is, you must now consciously, purposefully hold that picture in your mind of what you want the new you to look like. Hold that picture in front of you 24/7. See yourself at your desired weight. See yourself shopping for new clothes. See yourself wearing those clothes with comfort, satisfaction, and gratitude. It is truly not important how others feel about your accomplishment, but it is *vital* how you feel about it. FEEL it! Focus on how you will feel, how you will look, and how you will act. As in the discussion of the flower shop, think of all the details. See your life as it will be.

Your dream is your dream, and it is important, no matter the size or scope of it. The picture of it being accomplished is so very important in the process of bringing it about. Hold your dream in your mind. Revel in it. Live it as if it were already here. And then revel in the unfolding of it. *Allow* it be revealed to you.

Chapter 22
Positive Affirmations
Words Are Power

Affirm – latin for *ad-*, to + *firmare*, make firm   ("make firm to. . .") v. 1. to assert, 2. to confirm

All speech is an affirmation. Everything you say, be it true or untrue, is an affirmation sent to your subconscious mind. Remember our discussion of the subconscious; it does not judge the validity of input it receives. It merely records it.

You have always used affirmations, and they have always had creative power in your life and have caused you to form beliefs about yourself. But, you have not always been affirming what you *really want*, have you? Have you ever heard yourself saying, "Sometimes, I am so stupid!" or "I will never have enough money"? Is that what you truly want to feel, and is it what you want said of yourself or your future? Well, now is the time to become aware of what you *are* affirming for yourself. If you want to make changes, now is the perfect time to start.

We have already discussed thoughts and their power. We will now discuss what actually comes out of your mouth, what you *say* about yourself, others, and the world around you.

Everything you say is registered and recorded in the subconscious minds of both you and the listener. By the same token, words spoken by others also register in your subconscious. (Be careful who you choose for friends.) The statements you have accumulated in your subconscious have helped make up who you believe yourself to be.

You have no control over what others say, but you have total control over what comes out of your mouth. You have total control over what you wish affirmed for yourself. And if you want positive change, you have to become aware of what you have been affirming in the past. In the future it will be necessary to *consciously* affirm (state, declare, pronounce, confirm, assert, maintain) only what you *want* for yourself.

Positive affirmations have long been used for the purpose of changing thought patterns, habits, and personality characteristics. They are a powerful tool to use for change. When used with other tools of positive creation, they become even more powerful and effective. However, one must be very picky and choosey about the words one uses. If our word creates, we want our word to be positive. If, in the past, they haven't been positive, they can be changed.

Unfortunately, humans tend to be negative. We think and say negative statements without thinking, and that is the problem. We have to think about it; we have to be aware of our speech, at all times. In order to reach a state of happiness, we have to consciously think happiness, consciously speak happiness, and consciously act as the happy person we are.

As I have said, all words are affirmations, and the subconscious listens to and acts upon what it is told. Anytime you talk to yourself or others in any negative form, you are only reinforcing that which you do *not* want. For example, if you are not feeling well, keep your own counsel. Do not tell everyone every little detail of your disease or medical problem and how badly it is affecting you. Your dwelling on the idea of illness, and your innate ability to create what you think about, may very well be the reason you are sick. Negative thinking causes the body to produce chemicals that inhibit the balance of the bodily systems, and therefore can bring on *dis*-ease. Your negative thoughts, powered by your words, can delay healing. They can also cause your future experience to be more of the same. Your body will not heal itself if you continually tell it how sick it is and how much pain it is causing. No matter what false beliefs you have, that your thoughts have no power to heal, they are not true and can be changed. Release these feelings and false beliefs. Negative emotions and feelings cause almost all sickness. As hard as it may be to believe that thought heals, affirm to yourself, "I am perfect health." Or use the affirmation in the next paragraph. Both affirmations have been shown to facilitate healing.

In the 1920's a French psychologist and pharmacist named Emile Coue helped thousands of people in his free clinic heal themselves of disease, using only one affirmation. That affirmation is: "Every day in every way, I am getting better and better." He had his patients go into a relaxed state or meditation and repeat the affirmation 20 times, twice a day. People the world over still use this affirmation. It was re-introduced back in the 1970's by Jose Silva and used as a part of the Silva Mind Control Method. Coue's affirmation can replace any negative thought with a positive one. I use the same affirmation with a one-word change. "Every day in every way I am better and better." It is my belief that taking the word "getting" out makes the affirmation completely present tense and affirms that the "better and better" is already accomplished.

You will notice the use of the "I Am" phrase in Coue's affirmation. "I Am" is the most powerful affirmation to use.

Examples might be: "I am perfect health" or "I am peace." Everything is contained in one simple phrase and is easily assimilated by the subconscious mind. It is strongly positive. It declares what you *are*, not what you *want*. It is present tense, in the now. Always state positive affirmations in the present tense. It tells the subconscious it has already been accomplished, and the job of the subconscious is to bring this fact forward when needed. If you tell the subconscious mind, "I *want* perfect health," it will keep you in a place of *wanting*, by giving you the wanting you asked for. Research shows the subconscious needs to be given very specific instructions, the simpler the better.

Positive affirmations used with the other tools of meditation, emotional release, visualization, and gratitude can be very powerful in helping you create the life you desire. There is something you need to keep in mind when writing and stating affirmations. It has been found that the brain does not react well to the word "no." (That sure explains why children react the way they do to the word. It's just the way we're wired.) The word "no" disrupts the brain from what it is presently doing, in this case affirmations.

It has also been found that when negative words are put into what seem like positive phrases, those phrases become confusing to the subconscious; and a positive effect is not forthcoming. Use only positive words when writing or stating your affirmations. Refrain from using words such as "no, don't, never, not, should." Relinquish any feelings of judgment. Keep the affirmation simple. The more words you use, the more difficult for the subconscious to assimilate.

Example: Say, "I am at peace" or "I am peace." Do not say, "I am trying to find peace" or "I will find peace" or "I want peace." Trying and wanting are negative words, when it comes to affirmations. They tell the subconscious to keep trying and wanting, and you will never find what you are seeking. Even a statement like "I am no longer impatient" is stated in a negative way.

Here are a few examples of negative thoughts/feelings, followed by a few appropriate affirmations:

Anger:
I am agreeable.
I am calm.
I choose contentment.
I am full of joy.

Criticism:
I approve of myself.
I accept myself.
I accept others.

Fear:
I am love. It is who I really am.
I am in control.
I know there is a solution to this. I know it will come to me.

Frustration:
I am patient. All is well.
I choose peace.

Low Self Esteem
I am bright and resourceful.
I always know what to do.
I can be, do, and have anything I desire.

You can also use Coue's phrase, using words to your liking or that are the most appropriate for you. It has been proven to be a very effective positive affirmation over time.

- Every day in every way, I am better and better
- Every day in every way, I am more peaceful, patient, and serene.
- Every day in every way, I am calm and more content.
- Every day in every way, I am healthy.

- Every day in every way, I express more love and joy
- Every day in every way, I see the beauty around me.
- Every day in every way, I am filled with gratitude.

- Every day in every way, my financial state is better and better.
- Every day in every way, I achieve better and better grades.
- Every day in every way, I completely and deeply love and accept myself.

When doing affirmations you might want to add a tapping routine from Chapter 17 about emotional release. Every time you state an affirmation do the entire tapping routine, starting with the KC point. This will always clear your energy pathways when stating affirmations.

Practice your positive affirmations whenever you can and especially use them in active meditation. The point is to incorporate them into your thought process. Practice makes perfect, and persistence pays off. Don't miss an opportunity to slip in some affirmations. You won't have to stop what you are doing, necessarily. I find that repeating them while walking is an effective way to focus my mind on what I am saying. By focusing you can begin to get a rhythm going, and it becomes quite easy.

Just remember, it's important to focus on and feel what you are affirming. If you are out there to appreciate the nature around you, it might not be the time for affirmation work. Affirm and appreciate what you are seeing and feeling. Nature is always a wonderful place for expressing gratitude.

If you are persistent, you will discover over time that you quite naturally speak to yourself in a more positive way. How terrific that is! You are worth having those nice things said about you, especially by God (for that is who you are). Listen to all those wonderful things, and create a life of joy.

Chapter 23
Go With The Flow

"By letting it go, it all gets done. The world is won by those who let it go.
But when you try and try, the world is beyond the winning."
~Lao Tzu~

Asking for what your desire, thinking about it with love, and visualizing it as being exactly the way you want it, are all steps to creating what you want, whatever it might be. But, there then comes a time when you have to let it go. You have to release your desire to the Universe, to God, to the Power of Good. You can picture that as being a river. Set your boat in the water, get in, point downstream, and relax. Then, let your desire go with the flow.

God said, "Be still and allow Me to do whatever you want done." That is what He meant. It is now His job to bring about your desire. He knows how to do it. Allow Him to do it. It is your job to **believe** that He will, have *faith* that He will, and **expect** that He will. We hear much about that belief and faith part. But know that your expectation is so very important. Expect that you will see what it is that you desire.

As we humans are creating, and as we are waiting for our desire to manifest, we might have a tendency to be anxious. We worry about the results. We doubt. We can get angry in our impatience. All of these negative emotions are resistance and fear. If "like attracts like," resistance attracts more resistance, and fear attracts more fear.

If these negative emotions pop up, first thank them for appearing, showing you that you have a little resistance and a little work still to be done. Go within and go back to the process of emotional release. Let those negative emotions go. Thanking them may sound silly, but they are there for a reason. Being grateful will automatically put you in a positive place, allowing you to be kind to yourself. Releasing your resistance is a necessity and puts you back in the flow. Visualize that river, and picture you in your boat, happily anticipating your desire, which can *only* be *down*stream. Get up every morning ready to move forward, downstream.

Don't indulge in thoughts that letting go is going to be hard. What could be easier than sitting in your boat and going down the river? The river does all the work. Let it! Your ego might try to interrupt the flow. But you are strong. You have used your affirmations to assert your strength and resolve. Picture that strength and resolve as passengers in your boat, if you like. They will enjoy the ride, too.

Again, get up every morning looking forward to life. Love and accept everything you see and every situation that occurs. Thank it all for being part of your process. Keep your thoughts on God and your God-Self. Remember that strength and resolve. And keep that picture in your mind of whatever you have decided to create. The basics of creation are thought, word, and deed. Act accordingly. I realize this is a tall order. But, I speak from my own experience. Like anything else you want to do well, it gets easier with practice.

Here is a favorite song of mine, which I have always thought tells the whole story of how to live our lives. Pay particular attention to the bold, underlined words. Contemplate those words.

Row, row, row **your** boat
Gently **down** the stream
Merrily, merrily, merrily, merrily
Life is but a **dream**

Go with the flow. Don't resist. That is fear and can only attract more resistance. Let the flow (love) carry you along. I realize that to some this sounds somewhat childish. That's what I thought, too, until I found this is how life works best; and being childish is not at all bad. If you practice all that is positive, express everything in a loving way, promote kindness and harmony, and do your best to live peace, you become the flow. Positive emotions go with the flow, as it is their nature. When you become your nature, you cannot help but be in the flow.

Chapter 24
What Now?

Most humans have at least something in their lives they are happy about. Most of us have some things or, in some cases, many things that we are *not* happy about. We want to change these things. This is a common thread through human life. That which we are happy about seems to come easily and without a great deal of effort, almost automatically. But the things we do not have seem very hard to get. The changes we want, of course, are all as different as there are people; but the solution is the same. *Love.*

There are *four basic reasons* why most people do not have everything they want in life. My mission has been to show you ways to create that better life of happiness, joy, love, and fulfillment, things we all are seeking.

Reason #1: We do not realize who we are and the power we have.

Most of us, some 97% of the world population, believe there is a higher being in the universe, an intelligence of some kind. That Higher Being, that Intelligence, is Who We Are. I call it by the name of God, and Who We Are is God. You are God. I am God. God is the Source, and the Source is where you and your power, wisdom, and love originate. Source is, I believe, the energy I define as God. That energy is within you, waiting for you to use it for whatever you choose. When you realize (make real) the God-Self, who is *only* love, and learn to use Its power, your life will become easier, happier, and more joyful. The point of all this is to create a better life of total joy and happiness *now*, rather than later. Heaven on earth is *now*, not just in a promised future after your physical death.

Is it time for a new belief system? Is it possible that we have misinterpreted who and what God is? For thousands of years we have been told about who and what God is, and this does not seem to be working for us nor serve us well. Is it time to reconsider the rules of the game of Life? Is it time to ask ourselves if the human brain alone is the creative source and intelligence responsible for human progress and evolution? Are we really so arrogant as to believe that all the creative ideas for advancements in our life--cultural, technological, scientific--all come directly from a human brain? And as we look out upon our planet and our universe, are we so blind as to believe that within all the mathematical systems, all the order, and all the beauty present in everything, there is no intelligent guidance, that we are just one gigantic accident? I can't comprehend that to be so.

Could there be another answer? I believe in both KIS and Occam's razor; meaning, keep it as simple as possible, and the fewer assumptions and interpretations the better. Why are we here? Are we here to learn lessons or seek enlightenment, as so many say we are? That makes little sense. We already have available to us all the wisdom and knowledge of the universe. Why do we *seek* enlightenment, if we already *are* enlightenment?

Is it as simple as being involved in the largest stage play ever performed? God is the set designer, as well as the director and producer, so to speak. We are the characters, but with a big twist. We are also the creators of our stage parts, because we get to write our own scripts. We can create a script (life) of struggle, misery, death, and destruction; or we can design a life of happiness, love, and joy. We can do it *on purpose*. We can do it *consciously*. If asked right now, what do you choose? Your answer, without your stating it out loud, is revealed by how your life looks right now. You are living what you have chosen up to this point. That is true for each one of us.

We are perfectly-designed vehicles, unless we choose otherwise, used by God, as God, to experience life in a human physical form. Being God and one with Him, we get to choose the form and the environment in which we live our life. This is God's original idea, being performed perfectly.

To use this power, a better understanding of what that power is, and how it relates to each individual, is important. As I have said before, God is love. Simply stated, love is anything positive. In short and on a practical basis, love works; fear and negative emotions do not work. More importantly, the negative does not get you what you desire and, in fact, can cause physical and mental harm.

Understanding God, His power, wisdom, and love has nothing to do with religion or church doctrine and ritual. Having stated that, I believe churches to have mistakenly taught that their ways are the only ways available to really understand God. And they have often taught through fear tactics (the concept of hell).

True understanding of God has to do with how you live your life, what and how you think, and how you can create the life you desire. All of God's power, wisdom, knowledge, and love is within you. All the answers you need can be found within yourself (inherent). However, an individual can use this power, wisdom, and love in a religion and church practices if he/she so chooses; because God's power, wisdom, knowledge, and love are far beyond any religion or church yet formed, in our experience.

To re-cap, God does not ask or require that you do anything

your free will does not want to do. God does not judge you, *ever*. God expresses *only* love. He is love, that is His nature. He gives freely, unconditionally and impersonally, all the power, wisdom, knowledge, and love that He possesses. He plays no favorites. Everyone, everywhere is equal. Everyone, everywhere is God. He does not hate, does not get angry, is never disappointed, and threatens no punishment. In fact, He cannot express anything negative, *never, ever*, because that would go against His nature.

You do not have to join anything to receive all of the good you deserve. *You can* contact God at anytime for help and assistance. No matter what you have read, heard, or been told to the contrary, this is true. Accept it, believe it, allow it, practice it. You have nothing to lose and everything to gain.

Reason #2: We express fear, rather than love.

God is experiencing *every* facet of human life through us, both positive and negative. In your life, He experiences what you choose, because He gave you free will. If you are experiencing a portion of your life you do not like, it could be that you have previously burdened yourself with negative beliefs and emotions in that particular aspect of your life. In order to experience full happiness and joy, you must express full love to everyone and everything. You cannot express fear and love at the same time. These fears and negative emotions reside in your subconscious mind and cause you to believe that what you desire cannot come about. You unconsciously react to your environment by attaching to those negatives, thereby causing you to act in ways that are harmful to your spiritual advancement.

In order to overcome these longtime negative feelings and beliefs, you ideally need to be rid of them. Practicing emotional release is one way to do that. It is a simple method, which can rid you of negative feelings embedded in your subconscious for a very long time. I have released emotions from my childhood. After you have released these emotions you will begin to feel more free, less encumbered. If you couple emotional release with the practice of consciously expressing more love, what you want in life will come more easily.

You express love by thinking and acting positively on a 24/7 basis. If that sounds trite to you, then you are feeling resistance; because positive thinking is what it's all about. But, as I have said many times, life is a process. You navigate through it one thought at a time. When you find yourself reacting with anger, resentment, or other negative thoughts, shout out, "Thank you, God, for showing me my negative feelings and beliefs." You have just found those thoughts and feelings which are blocking your desires and holding you back from accomplishment. Those are what must be released, sooner rather than later. Learn to release them.

Reason #3: We don't make the decision to start on the journey.

Many people put up roadblocks before they even get started. They might *wish* for change of some kind but do not start making it, because they do not believe it can be done. Their negative emotions take over, always fear-based. Those emotions can be released, and thoughts can be changed, but at some point one has to start, whether it is through physical action or mental action.

Belief can start with success, either yours (experience) or that of someone else (observation). When automobiles first came about, most people could not believe they would ever learn to drive; but they did. Today, youngsters see others driving; and know they will be able to learn, too. Now it is totally accepted and believed. Create any life you can imagine, but you *must* start somewhere.

Reason #4: We give up too easily.

Giving up simply means returning to the negative side of your personality, letting the ego re-gain control. But there is a positive side, even to this negative. As you release negatives and express more positive, it is extremely difficult, and almost impossible, to ever return to where you were. When you start expressing love, or increase your expression of the positive, changes can begin quickly. You will never be exactly the same person again. Expressing love means you will *always* be better, even if it is only a little bit. Your spiritual personality, your soul, is never decreased. The soul only grows and expands. The more you express and share the love from within, the better your life will become.

*   *   *

Using the tools outlined in this book, take a thought, an idea, an intense desire for something you want and begin the process of creating it. Think about until it becomes an overwhelming desire. At first, choose something small. Make it something you can easily visualize and believe in.

You are God, and there is no changing who you are. However, if you need to, simply make believe you are God. You can accomplish anything. Keep thinking you are God; and, as God, you can do it. This is deliberate creation. Thought fills your subconscious mind with your idea. Discuss it with God. Act upon your desire, doing those things in the physical world to advance the idea forward. Get rid of negative thought and emotion surrounding this one idea.

As you release these negative thoughts and emotions, you will find your negative reactions disappearing, as well. As you release the negative, replace it with positive thoughts and emotions. Start expressing love and positive thoughts to others everywhere in your life. Do this at work, home, shopping, anywhere you are, even when driving or out walking. If you are alone, express them to yourself and God. Remember, this is between you and God. By doing so, you immediately begin the journey, which will increase your happiness and joy. With every loving thought or act you add to your life, the more you are *being* God. The more you become who you are, the more you become love. The more you become love, the more love you attract; and the more your positive desires will be realized.

Saturate your mind and actions with thoughts of love and the God within. Know that you are God. Think about being God. Visualize being God. Meditate that you are God. Affirm that you are God. Every time one of those pesky negative thoughts arises, thank God for it, and then release it immediately. Replace fear and hate with love. Replace anger with peace. Create the life you want, as God.

You and God are one. You co-create with God. As humans we are the nature of God, in physical form. This does not diminish the individual, which is you. It enhances the individual. Instead of being separate from anything in the universe, you *are* the universe. Instead of just saying you have unlimited, potential possibilities, realize that you actually *are* unlimited, potential possibilities. There is an immense difference between *saying* it and *being* it. Being God, from a human standpoint, is the *act of being* love, joy, and positive thought. To *be* it, believe you are God. God's love, your love, allows you to express being it. Love is your nature, just as it is God's nature. There is no challenge in your life or on the human plane that love cannot solve. This is the first minute of the rest of this life. What do *you choose*, love or fear?

To be love you must choose it.

Be still and **know you are God.**

Appendix I
Positive Emotions

Looking through this list of positive emotions can help you become aware of those things you already have that are good in your life. They could also serve as reminders of what you want to add to your present experience. You could use these positive words to build affirmations and to use when meditating.

Make use of these words not only in your thoughts but in your speech, as well. When you talk to family, friends, or co-workers, use these words to give them the feeling that you care and are a compassionate person. You can inspire others with just a smile or a kind word. It will make their life a little bit better and may help them feel more of these same emotions. We are much more than we believe we are. We have unlimited potential with infinite possibilities. Choose being God in perfect human form. There is nothing to lose and everything to gain.

Abundant	Accepting	Approving	Awesome	Believing
Blissful	Brave	Brilliant	Calm	Compassionate
Conscious	Daring	Empowered	Excited	Experience
Faith	Forgiving	Gentle	Happy	Healed
Helpful	Honest	Honorable	Humble	Humorous
Inspired	Joyful	Kind	Loving	Mindful
Motivated	Non-judging	Open Hearted	Passionate	Peaceful
Positive	Powerful	Prosperous	Relaxed	Respectful
Self Reliant	Spirit	Successful	Supportive	Thankful
Trusting	Understanding	Unique	Wisdom	Worthy

There are more positive words on my web site you can download. www.dan-keating.com

Appendix II
Negative Emotions and False Beliefs

The subconscious mind is programmed starting before birth and is the keeper of all beliefs and emotions both positive and negative. In this information we are talking about the negative storage. You can use the list below to help you figure out which negative emotions, feelings and beliefs you have to work on. When doing your list, from Chapter 16 Self Examination, look at each word below and feel if you have a negative emotion or belief connected to that particular word. Most of the people I have talked to immediately recognize a negative feeling when looking at the words.

Abandoned	Abused	Accused	Alienated	Alone
Antagonistic	Anxiety	Argumentative	Arrogant	Ashamed
Beaten Down	Betrayed	Bitter	Blame Others	Bossed Around
Cheated	Condemned	Controlled	Cowardly	Cut down
Criticized	Cynical	Debased	Deceived	Dehumanized
Defeated	Defensive	Defiled	Discredited	Devastated
Discarded Excluded	Discouraged Exploited	Disapproved of Failure	Disrespected Falsely accused	Embarrassed Fearful
Forced	Frightened	Guilt Tripped	Humiliated	Ignored
Inferior	Insecure	Insulted	Insignificant	Interrogated
Intimidated	Invalidated	Invisible	Judged	Labeled
Laughed At	Lectured to	Left Out	Lied to	Lonely
Manipulated	Misled	Misunderstood	Mocked	Obligated
Offended	Over-controlled	Over-protected	Over-ruled	Outraged
Persecuted	Powerless	Prejudiced	Pressured	Put Down
Rejected	Resentful	Restricted	Ridiculed	Scared
Self Conscious	Shameful	Shunned	Stereotyped	Suspicious
Teased	Terrified	Tortured	Trapped	Uncared about
Underestimated	Undeserving	Unheard	Unimportant	Unloved
Unsafe	Un-trusted	Unwanted	Violated	Worthless

Here is a short list of life circumstances that often result in trapped emotions: Read the phrase and feel what comes up. Normally if you have the challenge in the phrase you will get a quick strong feeling of negativity and you then can work on releasing them.

- Loss of a loved one
- Divorce or the end of a relationship
- Financial hardship
- Job loss and forced unemployment
- Home or work stress
- Miscarriage or abortion
- Physical trauma
- Physical or emotional combat
- Physical, mental, verbal or sexual abuse
- Negative self talk
- Negative beliefs about yourself and others
- Feelings of Undeserving of financial prosperity
- Feelings that you are not worthy of_____
- Feelings that you do not deserve_____
- Feelings of not being good enough to _____
- False belief that you are being judged by everyone.
- False belief that you will never amount to anything
- Feelings of humiliation when criticized
- Undeserved guilt feelings
- Guilt brought on by family or religious beliefs
- Your beliefs about money
- Your beliefs about love
- False beliefs about food and consumption
- Emotions underlying procrastination

- Feelings of guilt about relationship happenings
- Limiting beliefs about yourself
- Negative beliefs that you are not supposed to be that good
- Beliefs that success is beyond you
- Resentment toward yourself for lack of accomplishment
- Feelings of lack
- Feeling of being powerless in relationships or finance
- Feelings of being unloved or not being able to give love
- Feeling humiliated by family for not doing as they wished
- Feeling inferior to others

You can find larger lists on my web-site where you can download them. www.dan-keating.com

Appendix III
Illustration and Description
of Basic Tapping Points

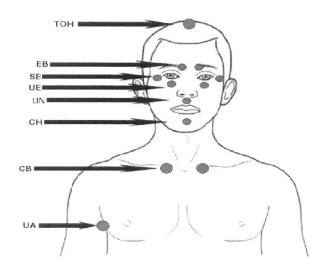

Karate Chop Point

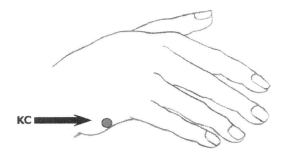

1. **(KC)** Karate Chop Point. This point is located in the center of the outside of either hand, between the wrist junction and the base of the little finger. When tapping, use all four fingers of the hand to tap point on side of opposite hand. Either hand may be used. (See illustration preceding page.)
2. **(TOH)** Top of Head Point. Point is located in center of head. Also called crown chakra point. (See illustration preceding page.)
3. **(EB)** Eyebrow Point. Where eyebrow begins just left or right of the center of the nose.
4. **(SE)** Eye Corner Point. Tap the bone at the outside corner of either eye. Both may be tapped at the same time.
5. **(UE)** Under Eye Point. Tap bone edge directly under either eye, or both at the same time.
6. **(UN)** Under Nose Point. Point is centered between nose and upper lip and centered under the tip of nose.
7. **(CH)** Chin Point. Centered under the lower lip in the dip between lower lip and upper chin area.
8. **(CB)** Sternum point. Directly below, about ½ inch, Adams Apple in U at top of breastbone. From this point move down one inch and right one inch. You may tap either side or both at once.
9. **(UA)** Under Arm Rib Point. At the point even with nipple on men and in the center of the bra on women on the side of the body. Use four fingers.

Tapping Tips

Some of the tapping points have matching points on each side of the body; for example, the "Eyebrow Point" (EB). Years of experience have shown that it is only necessary to tap one of these points. However, if you have both hands free, you can certainly tap on both sides for good measure. (See illustration preceding page.)

Tapping is done with two or more fingertips. This is so you can cover a larger area and thereby insure that your tapping covers the correct point. On points 3, 4, 5, 8 and 9 there is a point on either side of the body. You may use the point on either side, or tap both sides at the same time.

Tap approximately 5 times on each point. There is no need to count the taps, however, because anywhere between 3 and 7 taps is adequate. The only exception is during the Setup step, when the Karate Chop Point is tapped continuously while you repeat some standard wording. (This is explained in chapter on Emotional Release.)

The process is easily memorized. After you have tapped the Karate Chop Point, the rest of the points go down the body, starting at the top of the head (see the Sequence Points in the illustration on previous page).

Appendix IV
My Personal
Creation Examples

Although I have held the belief system you have read about in this book for more than twenty years, I have always had the belief that God existed. When I was a child, the belief was muddled and seemingly unimportant to me at the time. In my early adult life I paid no particular attention to God or the workings of the universe. I was, however, able to create a pretty good life, even with a major bump or two. My wife raised three great kids with a little help from me, but I was too busy trying to figure out what I was going to do the next day. Thoughts of God were fleeting, at best.

My first memorable encounter with God was on April 1, 1980. Up to that time I used a creative process I had learned from the numerous goal-setting classes I had attended. I did not attribute anything to God, or a higher power. I gave no credit to God for what happened on this particular day, until many years later.

April 1 is the official date I quit smoking. Smoking was the major cause of the medical condition I had experienced since I was 18. I had been trying to quit smoking for many years but was not able to accomplish it. Starting on April 1, I remember talking (praying) to God a lot. At the time I had been in the hospital for two months, confined to bed, with ulcerations on my foot. I repeatedly asked God to help me stop the smoking. I even used the foxhole prayers, "If you will get me out of this, I will never again . . . ." or "I will become a preacher, if you will just help me stop smoking."

When I returned home after surgery to remove four of my toes, the result of the infection and bad circulation, I was restricted to bed for another three months. After that, as I recall, I asked for help from God occasionally. I think at that point I rather forgot about God, but my life went on. I did get back on my feet.

But, I never smoked again and never had any desire or temptation to smoke. In later years, after I started my spiritual quest, I looked back on this April event, and gave God every bit of the credit (not that he needs or wants it). I realized how He had helped me with a problem I had been unable to solve on my own up to that point.

Upon examination of the event, I found I had unconsciously used many facets of God's creative process during that time period. I started with an initial positive *intention*—stop smoking. I spent much time in *prayer, asking* God for help, with the *expectation* that he would help. I expressed my *gratitude.* From that point on I *visualized* myself as a non-smoker and expressed aloud that I was a non-smoker. I had let it go and *turned it over to God*. I *released* the addiction and it's hold over me and carried on with my life.

Years after that April day, I learned that not one of my doctors had given me any chance of being able to quit smoking. I not only had peripheral vascular disease (PVD) but I was also diagnosed with Buergers disease. Buergers disease was said to be incurable, at that time; and the nicotine addiction associated with it was considered to be as bad as a heroin addiction.

My condition improved greatly over the next few years; and, I never again smoked. Nevertheless, some problems with my feet would periodically return. My condition had been in a very advanced state up to 1980, and poor circulation was still causing occasional problems. So, I began to create a cure for my PVD.

At that time, I was basically using the creative process more or less unconsciously. I had not yet truly realized how much power we have when we allow it to come forth. I believe that if I had known then what I know now, I could have accomplished the healing much more quickly. It took me about 15 years to get the disease under control and another five to eliminate it completely.

I used many aspects of the creation process that I had previously learned in my sales career. I used intention or goal setting, imagination, and affirmations. I did not use meditation and emotional release, however, two key factors I now believe are very beneficial.

My search led me to an alternative therapy called chelation. As I said, my disease was very advanced, so it took a great deal of this therapy to remove the blockages and plaque from my arteries and veins. Although for the most part I was unaware of it at the time, I now believe my God-Self led me to this information when I needed it. I was looking so hard and thinking about it constantly, and the information found me. As a human, when we are looking to solve large challenges, it can take some time; but it was certainly worth it, especially considering the alternative. (In my case, having my feet possibly amputated.) I now thank God every day for my perfect health.

*   *   *

I also used this creative process to find a new career in about 10 days time. For a period of my life, I was a real estate agent. I had reached a point when I realized I was experiencing far too much stress. I sat down and asked, "What can I find to do that can incorporate my given field and my experience?" I then started to look around town for opportunities. Long story short--within ten days I was led to everyone and everything I needed to facilitate my buying a sign company. This business fit the bill, precisely. I could use my real estate experience and contacts, as well as previous experience in marketing and advertising. I was able to quickly build this company into the largest real estate sign company in the region.

*   *   *

Here is an example of deliberate creation that I use all the time, and it takes less time to do it than it does to tell you about it.

Every year in the city where I live, there is a large street fair with over 100,000 in attendance. It is a 12-block affair in the popular downtown area of this college town. To say the least, there are not many parking spots within a half block of this event.

This last year, before leaving for the fair, I asked God for a specific parking space to be empty one-half block from the event. I visualized the space waiting for me. Then I thanked God for providing me with the parking space I desired.

When I arrived downtown I drove into a parking lot, turned right; and there was the space I had visualized. But it was not empty. I drove around the lot, came back to the street entrance, and looked at the space I had visualized once again. It was still full. There were dozens of cars driving around in the same lot. A thought came to me to leave the lot and go look down the street at the other end, which I did. I turned back the way I had come and went one-half block to a stop sign. My intuition told me to turn right. There on the street, space number two was vacant, but hidden behind a large SUV. The space was one-half block from the fair, just a block further south. As I looked back at the original space, it was exactly the same distance from the fair, almost to the inch. Thank you, God, for providing my parking space now.

If this was a one-time occurrence, you might think it coincidence; but it isn't. Creating parking spaces is a relatively small, but really obvious, result of deliberate creation. It increases my belief level greatly every time, and it is always fun to amaze family and friends. This same process, expanded upon, can create anything you wish.

*   *   *

I have shared these examples of events in my life only for the sake of showing you how you can change your life, whatever your challenge--health concern or parking space. You have the same power I have. I am God, and so are you. Have fun, and make your life a happy one.

Appendix V
Sources

Everything listed below I use, or have used, in the past.

Emotional Release:

Free Online Tutorial on EFT by Founder Gary Craig
http://www.garythink.com/eft
The Emotion Code, Dr. Bradley Nelson,
http://www.drbradleynelson.com/ Dr. Nelson's program is
primarily aimed at professional therapists.
Thought Field Therapy, Roger J. Callahan,
PhD, http://www.rogercallahan.com. This is another taping therapy.
Web Site Reading and Download about Lester Levinson, free
download of Levinson's story. Levinson learned to do releasing
by trial and error using the methods in this free download.
http://www.dan-keating/lester-levenson-story

Meditation:

Web site: http://www.massgeneral.org/bhi/basics/eliciting_rr.aspx
Simple instructions for the Relaxation Response by Dr Herbert
Benson.

Web site:
http://www.med.umich.edu/painresearch/patients/Relaxation.pdf
A free file with two simple relaxation techniques.
Dr. Joe Dispensa, http://www.drjoedispenza.com Inexpensive
guided meditations MP3 format.

Visualization:

http://www.naturalhypnosis.com This UK company has an MP3 file which has a guided visualization technique.
Starbursts: http://www.userlogos.org/node/5597

Books:

How God Changes Your Brain, Andrew Newberg, M.D. and Mark Robert Waldman
Emotional Release Therapy, Walter Weston
Relaxation Response, Dr. Herbert Benson, Meditation techniques
The Healing Energy of Your Hands, Michael Bradford
Breaking the Habit of Being Yourself , Dr. Joe Dispenza
Creative Visualization, Shakti Gawain
The Biology of Belief, Bruce H. Lipton
Jonathan Livingston Seagull, Richard Bach (as well as other books by Bach)
Life and Teaching of the Masters of the Far East , Baird T. Spaulding, 6-book set
Books by Esther and Jerry Hicks, Neale Donald Walsch, Dr. Wayne W. Dyer, Gregg Braden, Ernest Holmes, Eckhart Tolle, Eric Butterworth, Joel Goldsmith.

Made in the USA
Charleston, SC
03 January 2013